Unmasking the Devil

What the Bible Actually Says about Satan

Gage Coldwater

Deliberate Path Press

Contents

A WORD BEFORE YOU BEGIN

This book is not designed to frighten you. It is not written to produce obsession or paranoia about the demonic. It is written because the person who does not understand the Adversary is not safer for the ignorance. They are more exposed.

This is the first volume in a series of systematic theology aimed at young people. The word systematic just means ordered. Each book in the series takes one doctrine and works through what Scripture actually establishes about it, step by step, in a way that does not waste your time and does not talk down to you. The assumption behind this series is that young people are capable of serious theological work when the material is presented clearly and the Scripture is allowed to do its own work.

This volume is about the Adversary: his origin, his methods, his limits, his defeat, and what the believer is given to stand against him with. Thirteen chapters. Each chapter establishes one truth and hands it forward to the next chapter. By the time you reach the last chapter, everything you need to walk in victory has been put in your hands, piece by piece.

Every factual claim is backed by Scripture or a cited source. Check everything. That is not a disclaimer. It is an instruction. The Bereans in Acts 17:11 were commended because they received the word and then went home to compare it to the text.

Everything in this book is based on the King James Version. Where Hebrew or Greek words come up, they are given and explained plainly.

One more thing before you begin. In a few places this book will say "Scripture does not say." That phrase is deliberate. There are places where Christian tradition has filled in details the text leaves open. When you see that phrase in this book, it is an invitation to be careful. What the Bible says, it says clearly. What it does not say, we should not speak as though we know.

Gage Coldwater

INTRODUCTION

The Devil You Think You Know

Close your eyes and picture the Devil. Most people land in one of two images. The first is a red figure with horns, a pointed tail, cloven hooves, and a pitchfork. The second is a smooth, articulate character in expensive clothing who offers deals, quotes poetry, and is more interesting than the people around him.

Neither image came from Scripture. Not one feature of either picture appears in the Bible.

The first image was assembled over centuries from Greek mythology, medieval art, and folk tradition. The second image was invented by a seventeenth-century English poet named John Milton in Paradise Lost. Both have been so widely distributed for so long that most people cannot picture the Devil without reaching for one or the other, and both picture something that does not exist.

The point is not small. When you fill the space where a real Adversary belongs with a picture that does not match him, you are not safer. The person afraid of a cartoon is not afraid of anything real. The person fascinated by a romantic rebel has been moved by the thing we think we are only observing. Scripture calls this vulnerability by a specific name in 2 Corinthians 2:11: "Lest Satan should get an advantage of us: for we are not ignorant of his devices." Ignorance of his actual methods is an advantage given to him.

This book works through what Scripture establishes about the Adversary. It does so in order: first the heavenly realm he came from, then his fall, then his names and activities, then the false pictures, then his actual strategy, then his work against believers, then the powers arranged with him, then what Scripture shows about demonic beings, then the limits of what he can do, then the defeat already accomplished at the cross, then the armor the believer is given, and finally how a believer walks in victory.

Each chapter deposits one truth and hands it forward. By the end, you will know what Scripture actually says about the Adversary and what it actually provides you to stand against him. Start with that.

"Be sober, be vigilant; because your adversary the devil, as a roaring lion, walketh about, seeking whom he may devour: Whom resist stedfast in the faith." (1 Peter 5:8-9)

CHAPTER ONE

Before the Fall: The Heavenly Order

> *"In the year that king Uzziah died, I saw also the Lord sitting upon a throne, high and lifted up, and his train filled the temple. Above it stood the seraphims: each one had six wings; with twain he covered his face, and with twain he covered his feet, and with twain he did fly. And one cried unto another, and said, Holy, holy, holy, is the LORD of hosts: the whole earth is full of his glory. And the posts of the door moved at the voice of him that cried, and the house was filled with smoke."* (Isaiah 6:1-4)

Isaiah the prophet is given a vision of the throne room of God, and what he sees is a realm that is real, occupied, structured, and alive with worship but very unlike the world that we are familiar with. The Seraphim, whose name comes from the Hebrew word *saraph*, meaning burning or fiery one, do not appear as mere scenery in this realm. They are specific beings with specific features performing a specific activity. They have six wings apiece. Two covering the face, in reverence. Two covering the feet, in humility. Two for flight.

Before anything else in this book can be said about the Adversary, the Devil, this chapter has to be said about the realm he came from. Because most people think about the Devil without any picture of the heavenly world at all, and when they do that, they are often reasoning from a vacuum of mis-information. That vacuum is where the wrong pictures they have in their minds come from. Before the fall, there was an order. That order is where the story of the Devil begins.

I want you to notice something about Isaiah's vision before we go any further. The prophet dates it precisely. "In the year that king Uzziah died." This is not a dream or an allegory. This is a historical event placed on the timeline of Judah's kings. Uzziah died around 740 B.C. In that specific year, in a specific prophet's life, the veil between the visible world and the invisible world was lifted, and Isaiah saw the room where the decisions of the universe are made. When he came out of that vision, he was not the same man. A live coal from the altar was laid on his lips. He was commissioned as a prophet. And the rest of the book of Isaiah is written by a man who had seen, with his own eyes, what most men will never see until glory in Heaven above someday.

The Heavenly Realm Is Real

The first thing Scripture teaches on this subject is that the heavenly realm is not just a metaphor. Isaiah does not say he imagined this. He says he saw it. Other prophets describe the same realm with the same kind of directness. Ezekiel is given a vision of the living creatures and the divine chariot-throne in Ezekiel 1 and 10. Micaiah the prophet reports in 1 Kings 22:19 that he *"saw the LORD sitting on his throne, and all the host of heaven standing by him on his right hand and on his left."* John, in Revelation 4, describes a scene structurally identical to that in Isaiah: a throne, a figure on the throne, and surrounding beings worshiping without ceasing.

Daniel, in his vision of the Ancient of Days, sees something even more overwhelming.

> *"I beheld till the thrones were cast down, and the Ancient of days did sit, whose garment was white as snow, and the hair of his head like the pure wool: his throne was like the fiery flame, and his wheels as burning fire. A fiery stream issued and came forth from before him:*

> *thousand thousands ministered unto him, and ten thousand times ten thousand stood before him: the judgment was set, and the books were opened."* (Daniel 7:9-10)

A thousand thousands. Ten thousand times ten thousand. Understand this about this scene – the heavenly realm is not sparsely populated. It is not a thin place with a few scattered figures. It is filled, organized, and fully engaged in the service of the One on the throne.

Stephen, at his martyrdom in Acts 7, sees the heavens opened and testifies aloud before the crowd that was about to stone him. *"I see the heavens opened, and the Son of man standing on the right hand of God."* (Acts 7:56) Stephen was a dying man, filled with the Holy Ghost, and he looks up and sees what Isaiah saw and what Daniel saw. The veil lifts for him. The realm is there, and it is real, and at the moment of Stephen's death the Lord Jesus is standing to receive His servant home.

The apostle Paul adds another eyewitness account to this realm. He writes in 2 Corinthians 12:2-4 about a man, most likely himself, *"caught up to the third heaven"* who *"heard unspeakable words, which it is not lawful for a man to utter."* Paul is deliberately careful about the details. But he affirms the reality without hesitation or apology. The third heaven is a place. A man was caught up there. Words were spoken there that human language could not contain.

The point of piling up these eyewitnesses is not to overwhelm or even impress you. It is to remove a false picture that a lot of modern people have in their minds without realizing it. Most people in the modern West have been trained, often without anyone saying it out loud, to treat the spiritual realm as symbolic. Something poetic. Something psychological. Something ancient people said to explain what they did not understand.

The Bible does not treat the heavenly realm that way. It treats the heavenly realm as more solidly real than the physical world around us. When Elisha was surrounded by a Syrian army at Dothan and his servant was terrified, Elisha prayed a specific prayer. *"Lord, I pray thee, open his eyes, that he may see."* (2 Kings 6:17)

And when the young man's eyes were opened, he saw that *"the mountain was full of horses and chariots of fire round about Elisha."* The Syrian army was real. The chariots of fire were more real. But the servant had only been seeing half of what was there. We do the same thing as Elisah today – only seeing half of the image.

Stay in that passage for a moment. The servant's problem was not that the chariots of fire were absent. They had been there the whole time. His problem was that he could not see them with unopened human eyes. The terror he felt was proportional to his visible circumstances, not to the actual state of things. Once his eyes were opened, the whole picture changed without a single additional chariot arriving on the scene. This is the condition of most of the world most of the time. Not that the heavenly realm is absent. That their eyes have not been opened to see it.

Angels are real created beings. Colossians 1:16 establishes their origin:

> *"For by him were all things created, that are in heaven, and that are in earth, visible and invisible, whether they be thrones, or dominions, or principalities, or powers: all things were created by him, and for him."*

Thrones, dominions, principalities, powers. These are not poetic statements about the spiritual realm. They are categories of heavenly created beings with real roles and rankings within a structured order. The Hebrew word for angel is *malak*. The Greek word is *angelos*. Both of them mean *messenger*. The term describes what they do more than what they are.

Hebrews 1:14 states their primary function toward human beings: *"Are they not all ministering spirits, sent forth to minister for them who shall be heirs of salvation?"* Angels were created to serve. They are not rogue independent agents pursuing their own desires and purposes. They operate inside a plan of God that centers on redemption.

Think about what that verse is saying. The heavenly beings whose activity shakes the door posts of the temple in Isaiah 6 are, in some of their assignments, dispatched by God to minister to believers. Not to angels in general. Not to humanity in some vague collective sense. To "them who shall be heirs of salvation." If you have trusted Christ, you are not unknown to the heavenly realm. The same beings Isaiah saw are, by God's appointment, at work in the affairs of the saints.

Scripture illustrates this in several specific accounts. An angel shut the mouths of the lions in Daniel's den (Daniel 6:22). An angel released Peter from prison in the middle of the night, walking him through gates that opened of their own accord (Acts 12:7-10). An angel strengthened the Lord Jesus Himself in the garden of Gethsemane (Luke 22:43). Elijah, exhausted and suicidal in the wilderness, was fed by an angel twice before he could make the journey to Horeb (1 Kings 19:5-8). These are not isolated oddities. These are representative samples of what the heavenly host has been doing, quietly, throughout the entire history of the people of God. Most of it never makes the headlines. Most of it, you will not know about until the day the books are opened.

The Realm Is Ordered

The heavenly realm is structured into ranks, functions, and offices, including the Seraphim, Cherubim, and Archangels, illustrating a divine hierarchy that reflects God's order and sovereignty.

The Seraphim in Isaiah 6 are associated with the immediate proclamation of God's holiness. Their name, from the root meaning burning, suggests beings whose function is connected to the consuming holiness of God. They appear in this one passage, and their entire activity in that passage is worship. They cry "Holy, holy, holy" without ceasing.

Consider the posture of the Seraphim for a moment longer. Two wings cover the face. These are beings of tremendous glory, and still they cannot bear to look on the face of the One on the throne. Two wings cover the feet. The feet represent what has contact with creation, and even those are veiled in the presence of God. Only two wings are used for flight. The ratio is instructive. Four wings for reverence and humility. Two wings for service. If the highest of created beings come before God with that posture, then every picture of heavenly worship we give one another, and every posture we bring into our own worship, ought to start there.

The Cherubim are a distinct angelic order of their own. They appear throughout Scripture in connection with the presence and the glory of God. In Genesis 3:24, Cherubim are placed at the entrance to Eden after the Fall of Adam and Eve to guard the way to the tree of life. In Exodus 25:17-22, God instructs Moses to place golden Cherubim above the mercy seat of the ark of the covenant, the earthly representation of the divine throne. In Ezekiel 1 and 10, the prophet describes the living creatures around the divine chariot-throne. These seem to be the highest order of created beings serving in proximity to God.

Slow down with Ezekiel's description of the Cherubim. Four faces each. The face of a man, the face of a lion, the face of an ox, and the face of an eagle. Four wings each. Wheels within wheels beside them, full of eyes. The sound of their wings like the noise of great waters. Everywhere the spirit of God went, they went. Whatever God willed, they performed. There is no hesitation in them. There is no negotiation in them. They are service made visible. They are creation responding to the will of the Creator without friction.

Michael is named in Scripture as an Archangel (Jude 1:9). He is described in Daniel 10:13 as *"one of the chief princes,"* and in Daniel 12:1 as *"the great prince which standeth for the children of thy people."* Gabriel is named in Daniel 8:16 and 9:21 and in Luke 1:19 and 1:26, appearing in contexts of divine announcement. In Luke 1:19, Gabriel says, *"I am Gabriel, that stands in the presence of God,"* suggesting possibly a specific office in proximity to the divine throne.

Notice what Gabriel's assignments were, because they set the pattern for what angels do. He explained Daniel's visions. He announced to Zacharias the birth of John the Baptist. He announced to Mary the birth of Jesus. The specific messenger who carried the news of the coming of the Messiah is the same messenger who had carried the news of the seventy weeks of Daniel 9 five centuries earlier. These are the sorts of assignments given in the heavenly order. Not small errands or some random visits. Instead, they are sent by God in moments of redemptive history, carried by specific beings, from the throne of God into the hearing of men and women.

Michael's assignments sit on a different axis. Where Gabriel announces, Michael contends. He is described in Jude 1:9 as *"the archangel"* who contended with the Devil over the body of Moses. He appears in Daniel 10 as the chief prince who intervened to free the angelic messenger who had been held up by the prince of Persia for twenty-one days. He appears again in Revelation 12:7, where *"there was war in heaven: Michael and his angels fought against the dragon; and the dragon fought and his angels."* The office of Michael, wherever it appears, appears to be tied to the defense of God's people and against the operations of the Devil.

Scripture also speaks of *"the host of heaven"* and *"the armies of heaven"* and *"a multitude of the heavenly host."* In Luke 2:13, when the angel of the Lord announces to the shepherds outside Bethlehem that a Savior had been born, *"suddenly there was with the angel a multitude of the heavenly host praising God."* Not one angel but rather an enormous multitude of angels. The announcement of the Incarnation of Jesus Christ was not quiet work. It was the visible breakthrough of the heavenly realm into the fields of Judea for one night, and the shepherds witnessed it.

These are the specific named beings Scripture identifies by office. Most angelic beings in Scripture are unnamed. Scripture certainly is not exhaustive about the heavenly order. However, it is sufficient for us though. It gives us enough to know the realm is real and structured, without giving us a complete organizational chart.

Let me offer one caution before you move on. A lot of speculation has been written about the heavenly order over the centuries. Medieval theologians developed nine ranks of angels. Modern writers have produced detailed charts of angelic hierarchies. Some of these systems contain insight but honestly, most of them go well past what Scripture states. The line between what the text establishes and what tradition has imagined matters more than it first appears. Every time a Christian swaps out what Scripture actually says for what tradition has added, we become easier to confuse later. This book holds to the line of the text of Scripture alone. The realm of the angels is real. It is ordered. It has named beings with named offices. Beyond that, Scripture is silent, and we should be too.

The Realm Centers on Worship

The third thing Scripture establishes about the heavenly realm is its purpose. The central activity of the heavenly order, before anything else, is the worship of God.

Isaiah's vision shows this. The Seraphim are not strategizing. They are not patrolling. They are crying *"holy, holy, holy."* Revelation 4:8 shows the same scene centuries later:

> *"And the four beasts had each of them six wings about him; and they were full of eyes within: and they rest not day and night, saying, Holy, holy, holy, Lord God Almighty, which was, and is, and is to come."*

Day and night. Without rest. The worship of God is not interrupted.

Look at what the threefold holy is doing. In Hebrew, repetition intensifies. Saying something twice is emphasis. Saying something three times is the strongest expression that the Hebrew language provides. Of all the attributes of God, holiness is the only one Scripture raises to this intensity. We do not read that the Seraphim cry "love, love, love" or "mercy, mercy, mercy," although God is love and God is merciful. We read that they cry "holy, holy, holy." Because the distinctness of God, His otherness, His purity, His separation from every created thing, is the attribute that every heavenly being recognizes first and last.

Revelation 5 shows us even more of this divine scene. When the Lamb takes the scroll from the hand of Him that sat on the throne, the four living creatures and the twenty-four elders fall down before Him. Then the voice of many angels joins in. John writes,

> *"I beheld, and I heard the voice of many angels round about the throne and the beasts and the elders: and the number of them was ten thousand times ten thousand, and thousands of thousands."* (Revelation 5:11)

They cry together, "

> *Worthy is the Lamb that was slain to receive power, and riches, and wisdom, and strength, and honour, and glory, and blessing."* (Revelation 5:12)

The worship is not confined to the throne room. It spreads everywhere and very creature in heaven and earth and under the earth and in the sea joins in (Revelation 5:13). The whole realm, seen and unseen, is tuned for one activity.

Psalm 148:2-5 connects the worship of angels to the worship of the whole creation:

> *"Praise ye him, all his angels: praise ye him, all his hosts... Let them praise the name of the LORD: for he commanded, and they were created."*

This text gives some important facts for us to observe. The angels are created beings. They were made. And the purpose of their making, like the purpose of everything God made, is to give God the worship He alone deserves.

Job 38:4-7 adds something beautiful. When God answers Job out of the whirlwind, He asks him, "

> *Where wast thou when I laid the foundations of the earth? declare, if thou hast understanding."*

Then God describes the laying of the earth's foundations, and in verse 7 He says that at that moment *"the morning stars sang together, and all the sons of God shouted for joy."* The creation of the visible world was witnessed by the heavenly realm, and the heavenly realm responded with a song. This should help you picture the scale of what we are talking about. Every sunrise. Every stretch of ocean. Every star you have ever looked at. All of it came into being with a chorus from the heavenly host as the soundtrack, and that chorus has never stopped. This is a good place to also note that the heavenly realm had already been in existence when the world was created.

One more important observation before moving on. The worship of heaven is not reactive. It does not happen because God has done something new and the realm responds. It is something that is constant. It goes on day and night. It went on during the years the prophets lived. It went on while kings rose and fell. It is going on at this moment as you read this sentence. It will still be going on when the Devil is in the lake of fire and every visible trouble of this world is finally over. The worship of the heavenly realm is the steady baseline of the universe. Everything else is passing through. The throne of God is the still point of everything.

This is the realm Satan came from. It is real. It is ordered. It exists for the worship of God. Whatever he was in that realm, he was a created creature in it. Whatever function he held, he held it at one point as a servant of the One on the throne. Try, in your minds eye, to see him there, before the fall, taking his place among beings who do nothing but worship and serve the Almighty. That is the background against which the next chapter will be read. Because when you understand how much he had, you can then begin to understand how far he fell.

Why This Chapter Had to Come First

A lot of books about spiritual warfare start with the Devil. This one does not. The reason is simple. You cannot rightly understand a fallen creature until you understand the place and the order he fell from. If you start with the Devil, he becomes the center of the picture, which is the one thing he has always wanted to be. If you start with God on the throne and the heavenly host arranged in worship around Him, the Devil takes his proper place in the story, which is on the outside, having refused what every other creature in the realm was made to do.

The first truth this book wants to put in your hands is that the center of everything is the throne of God. Not the cross, though the cross is central to redemption. Not the Devil, though the Devil is a real Adversary. The throne. The figure on the throne. The worship that surrounds the throne. Every question about spiritual warfare, every question about temptation, every question about the Devil, has to be read against that backdrop. Because the throne is where the answer to every question begins.

What This Chapter Establishes:

One. The heavenly realm is real, not a metaphor.

Two. The heavenly realm is ordered, with ranks, offices, and specific named beings.

Three. The heavenly realm exists for the worship of God.

Four. Every angelic being is a created being. No angel is eternal. No angel is equal to God.

Review Questions

1. Isaiah 6:1-4 describes a vision of the heavenly throne room. What specific details in the passage establish that the heavenly realm is structured and occupied rather than empty or symbolic?

2. The Seraphim in Isaiah 6 cover their faces with two wings and their feet with two wings before they fly with two wings. What does this posture tell us about how created beings relate to God?

3. Colossians 1:16 names thrones, dominions, principalities, and powers as among the things Christ created. What does this verse tell us about the nature of spiritual beings?

4. The Hebrew word *malak* and the Greek word *angelos* both mean messenger. What does the meaning of the word tell us about the primary function of angels?

5. Hebrews 1:14 describes angels as *"ministering spirits, sent forth to minister for them who shall be heirs of salvation."* What does this verse say about the relationship between angels and believers?

6. The Cherubim appear at the entrance to Eden in Genesis 3:24, above the mercy seat in Exodus 25, and around the divine throne in Ezekiel 1 and 10. What does the consistency of their role across these passages establish about them?

7. Michael is named as an Archangel (Jude 1:9) and *"one of the chief princes"* (Daniel 10:13). Gabriel says of himself in Luke 1:19, *"I stand in the presence of God."* What do these named beings tell us about the structure of the heavenly realm?

8. Daniel 7:9-10 speaks of *"thousand thousands"* ministering to the Ancient of Days and *"ten thousand times ten thousand"* standing before Him. What does this picture of the population of heaven tell us about the scale of the heavenly order?

9. The central activity of the heavenly order, as shown in Isaiah 6, Revelation 4, and Revelation 5, is the worship of God. Why does this detail matter for understanding what the fall of Satan means?

10. Psalm 148:2-5 specifies that the angels were created. Why is it important to establish that angels, including the Angelic being who became Satan, were created rather than eternal, and how does this affect the way we understand the whole story of spiritual conflict?

REFERENCES

1. On Isaiah 6 and the throne room vision, see John N. Oswalt, The Book of Isaiah, Chapters 1-39, New International Commentary on the Old Testament (Grand Rapids: Eerdmans, 1986).

2. On the categories of heavenly beings in Colossians 1:16, see Peter T. O'Brien, The Letter to the Colossians and to Philemon, New International Greek Testament Commentary (Grand Rapids: Eerdmans, 1982).

3. On the Cherubim in Ezekiel 1 and 10 and their association with the divine throne, see Daniel I. Block, The Book of Ezekiel: Chapters 1-24, New International Commentary on the Old Testament (Grand Rapids: Eerdmans, 1997).

4. On the named angels in Scripture and their offices, see Sydney H. T. Page, Powers of Evil: A Biblical Study of Satan and Demons (Grand Rapids: Baker, 1995).

5. On Daniel 7 and the vision of the Ancient of Days, see John E. Goldingay, Daniel, Word Biblical Commentary (Dallas: Word Books, 1989).

CHAPTER TWO

The Day He Fell: Satan's Origin in Scripture

"And he said unto them, I beheld Satan as lightning fall from heaven." (Luke 10:18)

Jesus makes this statement to the seventy disciples after they return from preaching and report that even the demons were subject to them in His name. He says it calmly, in past tense, as one who literally saw it. Whatever else can be said about the fall of Satan, this much is certain: it happened, and Jesus absolutely witnessed it.

The previous chapter established that the heavenly realm is real, it is ordered, and it is centered on the worship of God. It established that angels are created beings. This chapter takes up the next question: when one of those created beings rebelled, what exactly does Scripture say about the event?

Here is where careful reading is so important. Scripture directly establishes some things about Satan's origin. It also leaves other things unstated. Christian tradition has filled in some of those gaps with what some consider to be reasonable interpretations, and some of those interpretations have been treated as if they were as certain as the text. They are not. This book strives to hold a clean line between what Scripture directly says and what tradition has inserted and inferred.

Why does this matter so much? Because the Devil has always benefited from confusion about his past. Every time a Christian treats speculation as a settled fact, we are more easily moved when the speculation turns out to be wrong. What the Bible says, it says clearly. What it does not say, we should not speak as though we know. The goal of this chapter is not to know less than we could about the Devil. It is to know, for certain, what we actually know, and to keep that separate from what we think we know.

A lot of bad teaching on spiritual warfare starts right here, with people making confident claims about the Devil's origin that go well past the biblical record. Some of those claims contain a kernel of something that is plausible. Most of them go so far past what Scripture states that they actually create a fictional history of Satan that functions almost like a rival Bible. A young believer who has absorbed that fictional history will find, when we look carefully at the text itself, that half of what we were told about the Devil and his origin is not actually there. That experience either produces a crisis of faith, or, if it is handled well, it produces a lifelong commitment to the practice this chapter is modeling: read what the text says, say what the text says, do not say what the text does not say.

What Scripture Directly Establishes

Five things are beyond dispute because Scripture states them plainly.

First, Satan is a created being. Colossians 1:16 says that all things in heaven and earth, visible and invisible, including thrones, dominions, principalities, and powers, were created by Christ and for Christ. Satan is not eternal. He is not self-existent. He is not a rival god. He was made, and what was made has a Maker. That Maker is Jesus.

This first truth is deeply important. The ancient Persians believed in two gods: a good god of light and an evil god of darkness, locked in an eternal contest neither could finally win. That belief system, called Zoroastrian dualism, has infected popular Christian thinking for centuries without anyone realizing where it came from. The Bible does not teach this. The Devil is not the dark half of a balanced cosmic coin. He is not the yang to the yin. He is a creature who refused to obey his Creator. One side of the war is infinite, eternal, and uncreated. The other side is finite, temporal, and was made from nothing.

If you grew up watching movies or reading books where the good and evil forces are basically equal and the whole story is about whether good can just barely hang on, please try to set that picture aside. That is not the biblical picture. The biblical picture is that God is everything and the Devil is a rebellious creature. The contest is not a close one. It never has been. It never will be.

Second, Satan fell. Luke 10:18 records Jesus saying it as eyewitness fact: *"I beheld Satan as lightning fall from heaven."* Whatever the details are surrounding the event, the event happened, and Jesus confirms it. Notice the word *"beheld."* Jesus did not infer this. He did not deduce it from Scripture. He saw it. The eternal Son of God, who was present at the creation of all things, including the being who became Satan, was present at the fall of that being. He is the perfect and ultimate eyewitness of this event.

The past tense also matters. *"I beheld."* By the time Jesus speaks this sentence to the seventy, the fall is already long accomplished. The war is old. Every human being who has ever lived has been born into a world where the fall of Satan is already history, not an ongoing event.

And notice the image. Notice the description *"as Lightning"*. Lightning is sudden and brilliant. Falling from a great height. When lightning strikes, it cannot be called back. It cannot be un-struck. Lightning is destructive and painful. Jesus's choice of this imagery is not accidental nor coincidental. The fall of Satan from Heaven was decisive, final, and beyond recall. Whatever the Devil was before that moment, he was something entirely different afterward. He did not fall halfway. He did not retain some partial glory that he is trying to rebuild. He fell like lightning. He fell all the way.

Third, Satan did not fall alone. Revelation 12:7-9 describes a war in heaven:

> *"And there was war in heaven: Michael and his angels fought against the dragon; and the dragon fought and his angels, And prevailed not; neither was their place found any more in heaven. And the great dragon was cast out, that old serpent, called the Devil, and Satan, which deceiveth the whole world: he was cast out into the earth, and his angels were cast out with him."*

Satan brought angels with him. They fell with him.

Revelation 12:4 adds a detail: *"his tail drew the third part of the stars of heaven, and did cast them to the earth."* If *"stars"* in this passage represents angelic beings, as many interpreters read it, then a third of the heavenly host fell with Satan. That is a lot. It is also not the majority. Two-thirds remained faithful. When Scripture names the forces of heaven, the host that did not fall is larger than the host that did. Remember that when the enemy's ranks seem overwhelming.

Another question is usually asked at this point. How could a created being, standing in the presence of God, persuade other created beings to follow him into rebellion? Scripture does not answer in detail. But it tells us enough to infer: the Devil was a being of tremendous presence and persuasive ability, and he used those gifts to draw others after him. This will come up again in later chapters. The ability to persuade is a gift from God. It was created as good. But in the hands of a creature turned away from God, the very gift that could have led angels in worship was turned to leading them into ruin.

Fourth, the root of his fall was pride. 1 Timothy 3:6 warns that an elder/bishop should not be a new convert, *"lest being lifted up with pride he fall into the condemnation of the devil."* That phrase, *"the condemnation of the devil,"* identifies pride as the specific sin that brought judgment on the Devil. Scripture does not give extensive detail, but it names the sin specifically.

Think about how much that one phrase tells us. Pride was the first sin in the universe that we know of. Not lust. Not murder. Not theft. Pride. And pride is what Scripture warns a Christian to watch out for above everything else when it comes to positions of leadership in the church. The sin that ruined the highest of God's creatures is the sin that will ruin anyone who lets it take hold. James 4:6 says *"God resisteth the proud, but giveth grace unto the humble."* The Devil's fall is not just his story. It is a warning stamped across the whole Bible.

Proverbs 16:18 says *"Pride goeth before destruction, and an haughty spirit before a fall."* That proverb is not just worldly wisdom. The Devil fell by pride, and every human being who falls into any other sin has passed through pride in some way to get there.

Fifth, Satan already existed before the events of Genesis 3. He appears in the garden, already in opposition to God, already willing to deceive. Revelation 12:9 and 20:2 call him *"that old serpent,"* directly identifying him with the Serpent in Eden. Whatever his fall was, and whenever it occurred, it was already accomplished by the time human history began.

That is what Scripture establishes directly and clearly. It is not a complete biography but it is a sufficient foundation. Five statements. Five certainties. A created being, fallen, who brought others with him, whose sin was pride, and whose fall was already complete before the first man and woman sinned.

A Word About Certainty

Before we go further, something needs to be said about how a Christian should handle partial information in Scripture. A lot of people, especially young ones, are tempted to pretend they know more than they do. It feels confident. It feels like faith. But faith is not the same as pretending to know unknown things. Faith is trusting God for what He has not yet revealed while holding firmly to what He has revealed.

Scripture gives us five certain statements about the Devil's origin. That is enough. We do not need to know exactly when he fell, or what his specific office was before the fall, or precisely how the rebellion was organized. We know who he is now, and we know enough about where he came from to make sense of who he is now. The rest is to be held lightly, with the humility that a mere created creature should have when talking about things only the Creator fully knows.

Deuteronomy 29:29 is the verse to remember here: "*The secret things belong unto the LORD our God: but those things which are revealed belong unto us and to our children for ever.*" The revealed things are for us. The secret things are God's. A Christian's maturity can be measured, in part, by how comfortable we are with that distinction. Immature faith wants all the answers. Mature faith knows which answers are available and which are not, and is content with the ones God has given.

What Scripture Does Not Directly Say

Scripture does not tell us when the fall occurred. It does not tell us the specific office Satan held in heaven before the fall. It does not tell us the precise sequence of events in the rebellion.

Two passages have been traditionally applied to the fall of Satan in an effort to fill in these details. Both deserve a careful look.

Isaiah 14:12-15 contains the passage that gives us the word Lucifer:

> *"How art thou fallen from heaven, O Lucifer, son of the morning! how art thou cut down to the ground, which didst weaken the nations! For thou hast said in thine heart, I will ascend into heaven, I will exalt my throne above the stars of God: I will sit also upon the mount of the congregation, in the sides of the north: I will ascend above the heights of the clouds; I will be like the most High. Yet thou shalt be brought down to hell, to the sides of the pit."* (Isaiah 14:12-15)

Before anything else is said about this passage, read the verse that sets up the whole section. Isaiah 14:4 says:

> *"That thou shalt take up this proverb against the king of Babylon, and say, How hath the oppressor ceased! the golden city ceased!"*

The chapter is explicitly introduced as a taunt against the king of Babylon. The king is called *"a man"* in verse 16. He has a physical body referenced in verse 19. The primary referent of the passage is an earthly king.

There is a fact about this text that is not widely known nor taught. The word *Lucifer* is not a name. It is actually the Latin Vulgate's translation of the Hebrew *helel*, meaning shining one or morning star. When Jerome translated the Hebrew into Latin in the fourth century, he used the Latin word *lucifer*, meaning light-bearer. The word describes the morning star, most likely a reference to the planet Venus, the brightest star in the predawn sky. It is a poetic description of how bright the king of Babylon had seemed before his fall. Calling Satan "Lucifer" as though that is his personal name is a translational problem and tradition, and it is not a biblical title.

Let me say it again. **Lucifer is not the Devil's name**. The Devil does not have a proper name in Hebrew or Greek in Scripture. He has titles, descriptions, and functions. He has the title of the Adversary, which is what Satan means. He has the title of the Devil, which means slanderer. He has the title of the Accuser, the Dragon, the Serpent, the Prince of the power of the air, the god of this world. None of these is his given name. It seems that the being was stripped of any name he may have had when he fell. Scripture identifies him by what he does.

Why has the Isaiah 14 passage been applied to Satan? Because the language of verses 12 through 15 appears to exceed what could be said of any merely human king. No human king literally falls from heaven or aspires to sit above the stars of God. Some interpreters have read the passage as describing two things at once: the arrogance and fall of the king of Babylon in the immediate context, and behind him, the original pride and fall of the spiritual being whose arrogance he embodied. Others have argued that the poetic language is simply hyperbole about an earthly king and does not refer to Satan at all.

Both readings have been held by careful, believing scholars. Scripture does not settle which reading is correct.

The honest position is this. Isaiah 14 is directly a taunt against the king of Babylon. It may carry a secondary application to the pride and fall of Satan. The parallels to what could be Satan's fall are real. But the passage is not given to us as a direct narrative of Satan's origin, and treating it as though it were is more than the text supports.

Look at the "five I wills" in the passage, regardless of which reading is correct. "I will ascend into heaven. I will exalt my throne. I will sit also upon the mount of the congregation. I will ascend above the heights of the clouds. I will be like the most High." Five declarations of self-exaltation. Five refusals of the creature's proper place. This is the anatomy of pride, laid out in five sentences. Whether these are the direct words of the Devil at the moment of his fall, or the words of a proud king whose arrogance mirrored the Devil's, the pattern is the same. Pride always wants what belongs to God, and it uses the word "I" a lot to get there.

Ezekiel 28:12-17 is the other passage. It contains language about a figure who was in Eden, who was *"the anointed cherub that covereth,"* and who was *"perfect in thy ways from the day that thou wast created, till iniquity was found in thee."* The chapter opens in verses 1 through 10 with a prophecy against *"the prince of Tyre,"* identified as a human ruler claiming to be a god. Then in verse 11 the address shifts to *"the king of Tyre,"* and the language that follows has been read by many interpreters as exceeding what could apply to any human being.

The same careful reading applies. Some scholars hold that the passage is entirely about the king of Tyre, using heightened poetic language to describe his arrogance. Others hold that the passage describes two figures, the earthly king and the spiritual power behind him, and that the descriptions in verses 12 through 17 reach past the human king to the fallen being who inspired him. The language of being in Eden as a created being before the Fall and of being "the anointed cherub" is difficult to apply to any human figure, which is why the second reading has been widely adopted.

But once again, Scripture does not settle the question. Ezekiel 28 **may** describe the pre-fall state of Satan. It may not. If it does, then Satan was a cherub of extraordinary rank, present in Eden, perfect until iniquity was found in him, and cast down because of pride in his own beauty. If it does not, then we have only the five direct statements from the previous section, and we know less about his pre-fall state than tradition has often claimed.

This book does not pretend to resolve what Scripture leaves open. It gives the passages, shows what they say and what they do not say, and leaves the question where the text leaves it.

Two New Testament Passages on the Fall

Two New Testament passages describe the fall of Satan directly. They add what Scripture actually states about the event.

Luke 10:18 has already been cited. Jesus says He witnessed Satan fall from heaven like lightning. Past tense. He was an actual eyewitness. Jesus does not explain the timing or the mechanism of it. He simply affirms that it happened and that he was there to witness it.

Revelation 12:7-9 describes a war in heaven involving Michael and his angels on one side, and the Dragon and his angels on the other. The Dragon is explicitly identified as *"that old serpent, called the Devil, and Satan."* The outcome is stated directly: *"neither was their place found any more in heaven."* They were cast to the earth.

The timing of this war has been interpreted in various ways. Some read it as describing the original fall before human history. What the passage establishes regardless of timing: there was war, Satan lost, he was cast down, his angels were cast down with him.

Two more passages should be give here. Jude 1:6 says: *"And the angels which kept not their first estate, but left their own habitation, he hath reserved in everlasting chains under darkness unto the judgment of the great day."* 2 Peter 2:4 says nearly the same thing: *"For if God spared not the angels that sinned, but cast them down to hell, and delivered them into chains of darkness, to be reserved unto judgment."* These two verses tell us something that will come up again in Chapter Eight. Not all of the fallen angels are currently active in the world. Some of them, because of specific sins not fully described in Scripture, are already imprisoned and awaiting final judgment. The Devil's forces are smaller than the original number of rebels. Some have been removed from the field.

This is the complete picture Scripture directly gives. Everything beyond it is interpretation.

The Scale of What Was Lost

Step back and consider what the fall of Satan actually was. This was not a minor malfunction in the heavenly order. This was the defection of a being of tremendous capacity, carrying other beings with him, into permanent opposition to God. If Ezekiel 28 does apply to Satan, he was "perfect" in his ways from the day he was created. Every good gift that a creature can receive, he had received. Every privilege that a creature can hold, he held. And he threw all of it away.

Why? Pride. A creature looked at what it had been given, looked at the One who had given it, and concluded that the gift was not enough. The creature wanted to be the giver. The creature wanted the glory that belongs only to God. And because God is God, there is no middle ground between submitting to Him and warring against Him. The Devil chose war.

This is the choice at the root of every sin. Every time a human being decides to be his own god, decides that the limits God has set are the problem, decides that what he wants is more important than what God has said, he is repeating the Devil's mistake. Pride is not one sin among many. Pride is the sin behind every sin. It is the internal move that makes every external act of rebellion possible.

And the remedy is simple to state, though hard to live. The remedy is the opposite of pride. It is humility. It is James 4:10: *"Humble yourselves in the sight of the Lord, and he shall lift you up."* The being who lifted himself up was cast down. The one who humbles himself, God will lift up. The gospel itself runs on that principle, because the Lord Jesus, who was in the form of God, humbled Himself to the death of the cross, and God highly exalted Him (Philippians 2:6-9). Humility is the road into the Kingdom. Pride is the road out.

Young people face this test in a specific way. The culture around you constantly tells you that you are special, that your feelings are the most important thing, that the rules that apply to other people do not apply to you, that your generation is wiser than the generations that came before you. Every one of those messages is an invitation to pride. Every one of them is the old tempter's old sale, dressed in new clothes. The young Christian who wants to stand in the world without falling has to learn to recognize the voice of pride and refuse it. It does not mean thinking poorly of yourself. It means thinking rightly about God, about yourself as His creature, and about the other people around you as creatures of the same God, made in His image.

What the Fall Did Not Undo

One more observation before we close this chapter. The fall of Satan did not break God's throne. It did not compromise His rule. It did not diminish the worship of heaven. Isaiah's vision in chapter six comes hundreds if not thousands of years after the fall. The Seraphim are still crying "holy, holy, holy." The realm is still ordered. The throne is still occupied.

Put this firmly in mind. The Devil's fall was catastrophic for him. It was not catastrophic for heaven. The heavenly realm kept functioning. The worship never stopped. The plan of redemption, which had been in the mind of God before the foundation of the world, was still put into motion on schedule.

Nothing the Devil has ever done has genuinely threatened God. Nothing he does now threatens God. Nothing he will do between now and his final casting into the lake of fire will threaten God. He has been a defeated creature since before the human race existed, and the events of the cross and the empty tomb made that defeat public and permanent. The end of the story is already written.

What This Chapter Establishes

One. Satan is a created being, not eternal and not equal to God.

Two. Satan fell. Jesus Himself witnessed it.

Three. Satan did not fall alone. Other angels rebelled with him and were cast down with him. A third of the stars of heaven fell with him, but two-thirds remained faithful.

Four. The root of his fall was pride, identified in 1 Timothy 3:6 as *"the condemnation of the devil."*

Five. Scripture leaves some details about the fall unstated. Isaiah 14 and Ezekiel 28 may illuminate those details through secondary application, but they are not given as direct narratives of Satan's origin. Careful believers read them as possible, not definitive.

Review Questions

1. Luke 10:18 records Jesus saying, *"I beheld Satan as lightning fall from heaven."* What does the past tense and eyewitness perspective establish about the fall?

2. The chapter compares the biblical view of God and Satan with the ancient Persian dualism of a good god and an evil god locked in eternal combat. What is the key difference, and why does it matter?

3. Colossians 1:16 says that all things, including invisible spiritual beings, were created by Christ and for Christ. Why does this verse matter for understanding who Satan is and who he is not?

4. 1 Timothy 3:6 identifies pride as *"the condemnation of the devil."* What does this phrase tell us about the root of Satan's fall? How does Proverbs 16:18 reinforce this picture?

5. Revelation 12:7-9 describes a war in heaven in which Satan's angels were cast out with him. What does this establish about the scope of the original rebellion?

6. Revelation 12:4 speaks of the Dragon's tail drawing *"the third part of the stars of heaven"* and casting them to the earth. If stars here represent angelic beings, what does this tell us about the proportion of heaven that fell and the proportion that remained faithful?

7. Isaiah 14:4 introduces the famous *"Lucifer"* passage as *"this proverb against the king of Babylon."* How does this introductory verse affect how we should read the passage that follows?

8. The word "Lucifer" is the Latin Vulgate's translation of the Hebrew *helel*, meaning morning star or shining one. What does the history of this word tell us about treating "Lucifer" as Satan's personal name?

9. Some interpreters read Isaiah 14:12-15 as referring only to the king of Babylon. Others read it as referring to both the king of Babylon and to Satan behind him. What are the strengths of each reading?

10. The *"five I wills"* of Isaiah 14:13-14 are examples of pride spoken aloud. How does this pattern describe what pride does in any creature, including a human one?

11. Ezekiel 28:11-17 describes a figure *"in Eden"* who was *"the anointed cherub that covereth."* Why have some interpreters applied this passage to Satan, and what is the limitation on that reading?

12. The chapter holds that Isaiah 14 and Ezekiel 28 "may" describe Satan's pre-fall state but are not direct narratives of his origin. Why is it important to maintain the distinction between what Scripture directly says and what tradition has inferred?

13. Deuteronomy 29:29 says, *"The secret things belong unto the LORD our God: but those things which are revealed belong unto us and to our children for ever."* How does this verse inform the way a young believer should handle what Scripture does not tell us about the Devil?

14. The chapter says pride is the sin behind every sin. How does James 4:10 point to humility as the remedy for pride, and how does Philippians 2:6-9 show humility in the life of Christ?

15. The chapter says the fall of Satan did not break God's throne or compromise His rule. Why is it important for a young believer to understand that nothing the Devil has ever done has genuinely threatened God?

REFERENCES

1. On Luke 10:18 and Jesus's statement about witnessing Satan's fall, see Leon Morris, The Gospel According to Luke, Tyndale New Testament Commentaries (Downers Grove: IVP Academic, 1974).

2. On the primary referent of Isaiah 14 as the king of Babylon, see Robert Alden, *"Isaiah 14:12-15,"* Journal of the Evangelical Theological Society 27, no. 2 (1984).

3. On the dual-reference interpretation of Isaiah 14 and patristic readings, see John N. Oswalt, The Book of Isaiah, Chapters 1-39, New International Commentary on the Old Testament (Grand Rapids: Eerdmans, 1986).

4. On the translation of *helel* and the origin of the Latin *lucifer*, see Bruce K. Waltke and M. O'Connor, An Introduction to Biblical Hebrew Syntax (Winona Lake: Eisenbrauns, 1990).

5. On the debate over Ezekiel 28 as a description of Satan's pre-fall state, see Daniel I. Block, The Book of Ezekiel: Chapters 25-48, New International Commentary on the Old Testament (Grand Rapids: Eerdmans, 1998).

6. On Revelation 12:7-9 and the war in heaven, see G. K. Beale, The Book of Revelation, New International Greek Testament Commentary (Grand Rapids: Eerdmans, 1999).

7. On Jude 1:6, 2 Peter 2:4, and the imprisoned angels, see Thomas R. Schreiner, 1, 2 Peter, Jude, New American Commentary (Nashville: Broadman and Holman, 2003).

8. On pride as the root of the Devil's sin and the remedy of humility, see Philip Edgcumbe Hughes, A Commentary on the Epistle to the Hebrews (Grand Rapids: Eerdmans, 1977).

CHAPTER THREE

Who He Actually Is: The Names and Titles of Satan

> *"Now there was a day when the sons of God came to present themselves before the LORD, and Satan came also among them. And the LORD said unto Satan, Whence comest thou? Then Satan answered the LORD, and said, From going to and fro in the earth, and from walking up and down in it."* (Job 1:6-7)

In the opening chapters of Job, Scripture gives us the clearest sustained picture in the Old Testament of what Satan does. He is present among the heavenly beings who appear before God. He has been ranging throughout the earth. He has been observing. The conversation that follows reveals that he has been observing one man in particular, and that he has a theory about why that man serves God. He is described as an Adversary, an Accuser, a figure whose function is to oppose.

The previous chapter established that Satan is a fallen creature. This chapter takes the next step. Given that he fell, who is he now, and what does he do? Scripture answers that question not with a single definition but with a set of names and titles, each one describing a specific activity. Every name Satan carries in the Bible is a description of something he does.

In the biblical world, names were not arbitrary labels. They identified essential character or function. When God gives Abraham, Jacob, or Peter a new name, the name signals a change in identity and purpose. When Scripture accumulates multiple names for Satan, it is building a portrait. Not a photograph. A portrait. Each name adds a feature.

A young believer who learns these names is given something most adults never receive. Most people are taught one image of the Devil and never go past it. The believer who has worked through this chapter knows ten of his titles, knows what each one means, knows how each one shows up in real life, and knows from the outset that the enemy who shows up in our own life will be operating under one of these descriptions.

Satan: The Adversary

The name Satan comes from the Hebrew *ha-Satan*, which means the Adversary or the one who opposes. In its earliest Old Testament uses, the word is not a personal name but a title describing a function. Numbers 22:22 uses the same word for an angel of the Lord standing in the road to oppose Balaam. 1 Samuel 29:4 uses it for a human military enemy.

In the book of Job, where the title appears most prominently in the Old Testament, the Hebrew consistently reads *ha-Satan* with the definite article: "the adversary," not a name. By the New Testament, the Hebrew title had been absorbed into Greek usage as a proper name, and Satan had become the standard designation for the being who stands in organized opposition to God and to the people of God.

The word Adversary is more specific than it sounds. An Adversary is not a random agent of chaos. An Adversary is an opponent with a strategy, a figure who understands the terrain and adapts to it. 1 Peter 5:8 says:

> *"Be sober, be vigilant; because your adversary the devil, as a roaring lion, walketh about, seeking whom he may devour."*

Lions do not roar while stalking prey. They roar to panic the herd and separate the vulnerable from the protected. The image is of an intelligent hunter who is not attacking at random but selecting based on observation.

Notice what 1 Peter says about the believer's response. Not flee. Not negotiate. Resist.

> *"Whom resist stedfast in the faith."* (1 Peter 5:9)

The Adversary is real and dangerous, but he is not unbeatable. He is a creature, and he can be resisted. The same passage in 1 Peter assumes that resisting him is something believers can actually do, with the resources Christ has already provided. That assumption runs through the whole New Testament.

Diabolos : The Devil

The Greek word translated "devil" throughout the New Testament is *diabolos*, meaning slanderer or false Accuser. The related verb *diaballo* means to throw across, to cast between people, to cause division through accusation.

When the New Testament calls Satan the Devil, it is describing his primary occupation in relation to believers. Revelation 12:10 makes this explicit: he is *"the accuser of our brethren... which accused them before our God day and night."* The Accuser does not rest. He operates continuously, bringing charges against the people of God in the heavenly court and in their own consciences.

Zechariah 3:1-5 shows the pattern at work. The prophet sees the high priest Joshua standing before the angel of the Lord *"and Satan standing at his right hand to resist him."* The Accuser brings a charge. The Lord answers not by defending Joshua's record but by changing Joshua's garments. The filthy clothes are removed. Clean robes are put in their place. The accusation is not denied. It is answered by God's provision of what the Accuser said was missing.

Lucifer : A Title Without a Text

Lucifer is not Satan's personal name. The previous chapter established this. It is the Latin Vulgate's translation of the Hebrew *helel* in Isaiah 14:12, meaning shining one or morning star, applied to Satan by interpretive tradition rather than by direct biblical naming.

The name has acquired enormous cultural weight through writers and artists like Dante, Milton. It has become a name rather than a description, a designation rather than a title. But its actual biblical content, whatever application one gives it, points to a former condition rather than a current identity.

This detail is not just historical. 2 Corinthians 11:14 picks it up:

> *"And no marvel; for Satan himself is transformed into an angel of light."*

The masquerade works because it resembles something real. Scripture says the being who became Satan presents himself as luminous, as enlightened, as an improvement over what God has said. Whether or not he was once literally a being of brightness in heaven, what he does now is counterfeit brightness.

The young believer who hears the name Lucifer should mentally substitute *"the being who counterfeits light."* That is what the title actually means. It does not refer to a glorious figure. It refers to a deceiver who borrows the appearance of light to make his deceptions effective. The popular romantic image of Lucifer as a tragic, brilliant, fallen hero is exactly what 2 Corinthians 11:14 is warning about. The disguise is the dangerous part. The person who admires the disguise has been moved by the very thing the verse warns against.

Beelzebub and Belial

The name Beelzebub appears in the New Testament when the Pharisees accuse Jesus of casting out demons *"by Beelzebub the prince of the devils"* (Matthew

12:24). The name derives from the Canaanite deity Baal-Zebub, the god of Ekron mentioned in 2 Kings 1:2-3, where Elijah rebukes Ahaziah for consulting *"Baal-zebub the god of Ekron."* The name has been rendered "lord of the flies", likely a mocking Israelite version of a title that may have originally meant lord of the high place.

The New Testament's use of Beelzebub as a title for Satan connects him directly to the domain of demonic activity. Jesus, in His response to the Pharisees, does not dispute the existence of the hierarchy they invoke. He disputes who is doing the casting out.

Look at what Jesus actually says. In Matthew 12:25-28, He responds with a logical argument. If Satan casts out Satan, his kingdom is divided and cannot stand. The exorcisms therefore cannot be the work of the Devil. They have to be the work of the Spirit of God. And then He says something staggering in verse 28: *"But if I cast out devils by the Spirit of God, then the kingdom of God is come unto you."* The exorcisms are not just acts of mercy. They are evidence that the kingdom has arrived. Every demon Jesus drove out was a public announcement that the rule of the Devil over human lives was being broken in real time.

The Hebrew word *belial* means worthlessness, wickedness, or one who brings ruin. In the Old Testament, it appears as a description of wicked people, rendered *"sons of Belial"* in Judges 19:22. In 2 Corinthians 6:15, Paul uses it as a direct title for Satan in contrast to Christ: *"And what concord hath Christ with Belial?"* The name signals the complete absence of anything honorable or trustworthy. There is no common ground, no shared enterprise, no middle position between the One whose name is above every name and the one whose name means worthlessness.

This is a useful corrective for the romantic portrayal of the Devil that runs through modern entertainment. The Devil is not a rebel with style. He is not a charming villain with a point of view. He is *Belial*. He is worthlessness. The closer you look at him, the less there is to look at. There is nothing of substance underneath the disguise. That is what the name announces.

The Prince of the Power of the Air

Ephesians 2:2 gives a precise description of Satan's current domain:

> *"Wherein in time past ye walked according to the course of this world, according to the prince of the power of the air, the spirit that now worketh in the children of disobedience."*

The title identifies him as the ruling spiritual authority over the domain of the fallen world. The *"air"* in the ancient world was understood as the realm between heaven and earth, the space in which spiritual beings operate.

Paul's point in this passage is not primarily cosmological. His point is about what happens to human beings apart from Christ. People who have not been living according to Gods standard are said by God to be walking, "according to" the course directed by this prince. They are living, without knowing it, in alignment with the agenda of the one who rules the fallen order.

This is why the gospel is not primarily just a spiritual improvement. It is a rescue from a domain. Colossians 1:13 uses the same picture from the other side:

> *"Who hath delivered us from the power of darkness, and hath translated us into the kingdom of his dear Son."*

Transferred from one jurisdiction to another.

Think about how that changes the way you read every conversation about evangelism. Sharing the gospel is not just inviting someone to a better moral life or a more meaningful spirituality. It is announcing to a captive that the gates have been unlocked. It is telling a person who has been walking in alignment with the Devil's agenda for their entire conscious life that there is a way out. That is bigger than most evangelism is taught to be. The conversation is for higher stakes than people realize. Every unbeliever you know is, in Paul's language, walking according to the prince of the power of the air. The gospel is the announcement that the rescue has arrived.

The God of This World

2 Corinthians 4:4 uses even stronger language:

> *"the god of this world hath blinded the minds of them which believe not, lest the light of the glorious gospel of Christ, who is the image of God, should shine unto them."*

Satan is called *"the god of this world"* not because he is actually divine, but because fallen human beings have in practice organized their lives around his agenda.

His influence on the structures of thought, culture, and value in the fallen world has been so pervasive that Paul can describe him as functionally governing the minds of the unbelieving. The title does not claim that Satan has the attributes of deity. It describes the operational position he holds in the fallen world until Christ's kingdom comes in its fullness.

The Devil is called the god of this world, but he is not God. He has functional influence over a fallen system, but he does not have the attributes of deity. The title is descriptive, not metaphysical. He functions like a god to the unbelieving because the unbelieving have given themselves over to his agenda. The believer, who has been transferred into the kingdom of Christ, has been removed from his jurisdiction. He is no longer our god. He is the deposed authority we have been delivered from.

The Father of Lies

John 8:44 is Jesus speaking directly about Satan to the Pharisees:

> *"Ye are of your father the devil, and the lusts of your father ye will do. He was a murderer from the beginning, and abode not in the truth, because there is no truth in him. When he speaketh a lie, he speaketh of his own: for he is a liar, and the father of it."*

The phrase father of lies does not merely mean that Satan tells lies. It means that deception is his native language. There is no truth in him, not because truth has been expelled, but because he abandoned it. He originated the pattern that every lie since has followed: the substitution of a distorted good for a real one, the promise of wisdom or freedom or significance that produces the opposite of what it promises.

The title is also a warning about method. Satan does not primarily attack the believer with obvious evil. He attacks with plausible alternatives. The most effective lie is not the one that is obviously false but the one close enough to the truth to be believed. The Pharisees in John 8 were not obvious villains. They were seriously religious men doing what they believed was right. Jesus tells them they are operating from their father's agenda without knowing it.

Read that again. Religious men, doing what they believed was right, operating from the Devil's agenda without knowing it. That is one of the more sobering sentences in the New Testament. Sincerity is not the same thing as truth. A person can be deeply convinced they are doing the right thing and be operating from the wrong source. The test is not how strongly we feel about it. The test is whether what we are doing aligns with what God has actually said. The Pharisees failed that test. Anyone can fail it. The way to not fail it is to keep going back to the Word of God as the standard, instead of trusting the depth of one's own conviction.

The other thing the father-of-lies title carries is the genealogy of every lie. When you hear something false, you are listening, in some sense, to a descendant of the original lie in the garden. The Devil's offspring are everywhere, and they all have the same family resemblance: they put a question mark on what God has said, they minimize the consequences of disobedience, and they present the forbidden as if it were a higher good. The Devil is the father of lies. Every lie that has ever been told has his fingerprints on it.

The Murderer from the Beginning

John 8:44 also calls Satan *"a murderer from the beginning."* This title carries the weight of what the Devil's deception in the garden actually accomplished. He told Adam and Eve they would not surely die. They believed him. They died. Spiritually, immediately. Physically, eventually. Every human death since then traces back to that moment. The Devil is called a murderer not because he wields a weapon but because he introduced the condition that produces death.

This is also why the cross has the central place it does in the answer to the Devil. Hebrews 2:14 says that Christ took on flesh and blood *"that through death he might destroy him that had the power of death, that is, the devil."* The murderer was answered by the Lamb who allowed Himself to be killed and then walked out of the tomb three days later. The instrument the Devil used to hold humanity in fear was used against him. The way of death was turned into the way of life.

The murderer title also gives you a way to read what is happening when destructive choices are presented to you as freedom. The Devil's offers always end in death of some kind. Sometimes it is the death of a relationship. Sometimes the death of a future. Sometimes physical death. He is running a killing field, and the bait he uses is whatever looks most attractive at the moment. Recognize the pattern. He kills what he can.

The Roaring Lion and the Ancient Serpent

1 Peter 5:8 gives the last title for this chapter:

> *"Be sober, be vigilant; because your adversary the devil, as a roaring lion, walketh about, seeking whom he may devour."*

And Revelation 12:9 and 20:2 call him *"that old serpent."* The two images represent two modes of attack.

The lion attacks openly: accusation, direct assault, persecution. The Serpent attacks quietly: subtlety, guile, the question that plants doubt. Both require a different kind of attention. The lion requires courage. The Serpent requires discernment. The same Adversary uses both modes depending on which will be more effective.

Taken together, these names paint a portrait of an Adversary who is real, intelligent, strategic, and specifically oriented against the people of God and the purposes of God. He opposes. He accuses. He deceives. He blinds. He rules the fallen order. He murders. He devours. None of these activities is metaphorical. All of them have been experienced by humans throughout history. The names are a field guide, written by the One who knows the Adversary better than anyone.

Notice one more thing about the lion image. Peter says the Devil walks about "seeking" whom he may devour. The verb implies looking, evaluating, selecting. He does not devour at random. He targets. He picks the most vulnerable, the most isolated, the most distracted. That is why Peter's instruction begins with two commands: "Be sober, be vigilant." Sober means not numbed by anything that would dull your awareness. Vigilant means actively watching. The lion is real. The lion is hunting. The believer who is sober and vigilant is not the easy target the lion is looking for.

The Serpent image carries something different. The Serpent in Genesis 3 was not loud. He did not roar. He spoke quietly. He asked a question. He waited for the answer to take root. That is the Devil's other mode, and many believers underestimate it. The roar is easier to recognize because it is loud. The whisper is harder because it sounds like your own thoughts. The Christian who has learned only to brace against the roar will be defenseless against the whisper. Both modes are real. Both require resistance. The same enemy uses both.

How Knowing the Names Helps

A young believer might ask why all of this matters in actual daily living. The answer is in 2 Corinthians 2:11:

> *"Lest Satan should get an advantage of us: for we are not ignorant of his devices."*

Knowing the names means not being ignorant of his devices. Each title points to a specific thing that he does. When you face that specific thing, you can name it for what it is, and naming a deception accurately is half the battle of resisting it.

What This Chapter Establishes

One. Every name Satan carries in Scripture describes an activity.

Two. He is Adversary, Accuser, Deceiver, Blinder, ruler of the fallen order, murderer, and devourer. The list is cumulative.

Three. His methods include both direct assault (the lion) and subtle deception (the Serpent).

Four. His influence on the fallen world is real enough that Scripture calls him the prince of the power of the air and the god of this world. These titles describe his operational position, not his metaphysical status.

Five. Knowing the names is equipment, not just theology. The believer who knows what the Devil does can recognize him when he shows up.

Review Questions

1. Job 1:6-7 shows Satan presenting himself among *"the sons of God"* and describing his activity as *"going to and fro in the earth."* What does this scene tell us about his access to the heavenly court and his activity on earth?

2. The Hebrew *ha-Satan* means "the adversary" and functions as a title in Job 1. What does the use of a title rather than a personal name suggest about how the Old Testament understands this being?

3. The Greek word *diabolos* means slanderer or false Accuser. How does Revelation 12:10 show this title in action?

4. Zechariah 3:1-5 shows Satan at Joshua's right hand *"to resist him."* How does God answer the accusation, and what does this pattern tell us about the gospel's answer to accusation?

5. The chapter distinguishes between the Holy Spirit's conviction, which leads to repentance, and the Accuser's voice, which leads to despair. What does this distinction mean for how a believer should evaluate accusatory thoughts?

6. The chapter states that *"Lucifer is not Satan's personal name."* What is the actual meaning and origin of the word, and what does 2 Corinthians 11:14 add to the tradition?

7. In Matthew 12:28, Jesus says, *"if I cast out devils by the Spirit of God, then the kingdom of God is come unto you."* What does this verse tell us about the meaning of the exorcisms in the Gospels?

8. The Hebrew word *belial* means worthlessness or one who brings ruin. How does this title correct the romantic portrayal of the Devil that runs through modern entertainment?

9. Ephesians 2:2 calls Satan *"the prince of the power of the air, the spirit that now worketh in the children of disobedience."* What does this title tell us about the condition of people living apart from Christ?

10. Colossians 1:13 says God has *"delivered us from the power of darkness, and hath translated us into the kingdom of his dear Son."* How does this verse describe what happens at conversion, and how does it relate to Satan's title as god of this world?

11. 2 Corinthians 4:4 calls Satan *"the god of this world."* What does this title mean, and what does it not mean?

12. Jesus says in John 8:44 that Satan *"abode not in the truth, because there is no truth in him."* What does this statement tell us about how Satan operates, and why are the most effective lies close to the truth?

13. John 8:44 also calls Satan *"a murderer from the beginning."* How does this title connect to the events of Genesis 3, and how is it answered by Hebrews 2:14?

14. The chapter describes two modes of attack: the roaring lion (1 Peter 5:8) and the ancient Serpent (Revelation 12:9). What does each mode look like, and what does each require from the believer?

15. The chapter says the names are "equipment, not just theology." How does knowing the names help a believer recognize the Devil's activity in real life?

REFERENCES

1. On the Hebrew *ha-Satan* as a title rather than a personal name in Job 1-2, see John E. Hartley, The Book of Job, New International Commentary on the Old Testament (Grand Rapids: Eerdmans, 1988).

2. On *diabolos* and its background in Greek usage, see Gerhard Kittel and Gerhard Friedrich, eds., Theological Dictionary of the New Testament, trans. Geoffrey Bromiley (Grand Rapids: Eerdmans, 1964-1976).

3. On the titles of Satan in the New Testament, see Sydney H. T. Page, Powers of Evil: A Biblical Study of Satan and Demons (Grand Rapids: Baker, 1995).

4. On Zechariah 3 as a pattern for the gospel's answer to accusation, see Joyce G. Baldwin, Haggai, Zechariah, Malachi, Tyndale Old Testament Commentaries (Downers Grove: IVP Academic, 1972).

5. On Matthew 12:28 and the kingdom of God in the exorcisms, see D. A. Carson, Matthew, Expositor's Bible Commentary (Grand Rapids: Zondervan, 1984).

6. On Ephesians 2:2 and the prince of the power of the air, see Andrew T. Lincoln, Ephesians, Word Biblical Commentary (Dallas: Word Books, 1990).

CHAPTER FOUR

The Devil We Invented

"Now the serpent was more subtil than any beast of the field which the LORD God had made. And he said unto the woman, Yea, hath God said, Ye shall not eat of every tree of the garden?" (Genesis 3:1)

Here is the first biblical appearance of the Adversary acting interacting directly with a human being. Notice what the text says and does not say. The Serpent is subtle. He is more subtle than any beast of the field. He speaks. He asks a question. What the text does not say is anything about horns, hooves, red skin, a pitchfork, a tail, or any of the visual features most people associate with the Devil. None of those details appear here. None of them appear anywhere else in Scripture. They were added later, by other extra secular sources.

The previous chapter established that Scripture gives us a set of names and functions that paint a portrait of the Adversary. This chapter takes up the question of why most people do not carry that biblical portrait. Instead, they carry an image assembled from sources outside Scripture. From Greek mythology. From medieval art. From poetry. From film. An inaccurate picture of the Adversary is a defense vulnerability. If what you fear does not exist, your fear provides no protection against what does.

Why give a whole chapter to clearing out false images? Because the false images are doing real damage. The person who carries the wrong picture in our heads will be looking for the wrong enemy. We will be on guard against horns and miss the suit.

We will be watching for monsters and miss the polished teacher. The Devil thrives on the inaccurate picture, because every minute the believer spends watching for what does not exist is a minute he can spend on what does exist. Clearing out the false image is not optional. It is the foundation for everything else.

The Horns and the Hooves

The horns, the cloven hooves, and the animal features of the popular Devil image did not come from the Bible. They came from Greek and Roman mythology, specifically from Pan, the god of nature, wild places, flocks, and fertility. Pan was depicted as half-man and half-goat, with goat legs, goat horns, and goat features. The Roman equivalent was Faunus, similarly goat-like.

Pan - The god of Nature

As Christianity spread through the Roman Empire and then through northern Europe, it encountered these nature gods. One of the strategies early Christianity used to delegitimize pagan religion was to identify pagan gods with demons. Those who had been worshipped as deities were actually fallen spiritual beings receiving worship that belonged to God alone. The apostle Paul had already moved in this direction in 1 Corinthians 10:20, where he says the things Gentiles sacrifice *"they sacrifice to devils, and not to God."*

The visual result was predictable. If Pan was demonic, and Pan looked like a goat-man, then depictions of demonic beings began to acquire Pan's features. The horns migrated from Pan to the generic demon. The cloven hooves and animalistic features followed. By the high Middle Ages, the standard artistic depiction of a demon in Christian art owed far more to the god of the Greek forest than to anything in the text of Scripture.

There was a strategic reason for the migration that is easy to miss. By making the old pagan gods look monstrous, medieval artists were trying to undo the appeal those gods had once held. A statue of Pan in a Greek temple looked attractive. The same figure painted on a church wall, looking demonic and grotesque, was meant to repel. The intention was good. The unintended consequence was that, over centuries, a generation grew up assuming that the monster on the church wall was what the Bible had been describing all along. The intermediate step, that Pan-derived imagery had been imported as a polemical strategy, was forgotten. The image stayed. The reasoning behind it disappeared.

The Pitchfork and the Red Skin

The pitchfork has no biblical origin. It derives from the trident of Poseidon and from implements associated with the god of the underworld in classical mythology. As Hades became conflated with the Christian concept of hell in popular imagination, the implement followed. Medieval artists depicted demons in hell using pitchforks to torment the damned. The tool became the weapon, the weapon became the symbol, the symbol became the universal identifier. Not one verse of Scripture puts a pitchfork in Satan's hand.

The color red is not assigned to Satan in Scripture. Its association with the Devil appears to originate partly from a sixth-century mosaic in the Basilica of Sant'Apollinare Nuovo in Ravenna, Italy, which depicts the Last Judgment scene from Matthew 25. In the mosaic, an angel in red stands behind the goats, associated with the condemned. Over the centuries, red became associated with hellfire, then with the Devil himself.

Mosaic in the Basilica of Sant'Apollinare Nuovo in Ravenna, Italy

By the late medieval period, the popular image of the Devil had been assembled. Horns from Pan. Hooves from Pan. Pitchfork from Hades. Red from medieval artistic convention. Tail added to complete the visual. None of it came from Scripture.

Here is something to notice. Every element of the image came from somewhere, and every element had a purpose at the time it was added. The purpose was to make the Devil look frightening to the people of that era. But what frightened a medieval European is not what would frighten you. The image that was designed to terrify a fourteenth-century peasant is exactly the image a twenty-first-century young person finds laughable. Costume parties. Cartoons. Halloween decorations. The image has lost its scare and become a joke. And the Devil is fine with that, because a Devil who has been turned into a joke is a Devil people no longer take seriously.

Dante's Frozen Monster

In the early fourteenth century, the Italian poet Dante Alighieri wrote The Divine Comedy, the most influential work of religious imagination in Western history. The picture of the Devil Dante painted shaped Christian popular imagination for centuries.

Dante's Inferno

Dante's Satan appears in Canto XXXIV of the Inferno. He is a three-headed giant frozen from the waist down in a lake of ice at the lowest point of hell. His three mouths chew endlessly on Judas, Brutus, and Cassius. His wings beat constantly and create the cold wind that freezes the ice that imprisons him. He is mute, weeping, and pathetic. He is not the ruler of hell. He is its most pitiable prisoner.

In some ways this portrait is more theologically honest than the later popular image. Dante's Satan is powerless, imprisoned, self-defeating. The wings that were supposed to lift him toward divine glory churn the wind that freezes him in place. His rebellion is his cage. This is not far from Revelation 20:10.

But Dante's Satan has a problem. He is so grotesque and so obviously destroyed that he is no longer frightening in the way the biblical Adversary requires a believer to be watchful. You do not fear something that pathetic. You pity it or dismiss it. Neither prepares you to "resist the devil steadfast in the faith."

There is also a theological worry hidden inside Dante's portrait. By placing the Devil at the lowest point of hell, frozen and powerless, Dante implies that the Devil is already where the Bible says he is going to be. But Scripture does not put the Devil in hell yet. Scripture says he is currently active. He walks about as a roaring lion. He is the prince of the power of the air. He still works in the children of disobedience. The lake of fire is his future destination, not his current address. Dante's image, interesting as it is, has the timing wrong. It encourages the reader to imagine the Devil as already neutralized. He is not. He is constrained, defeated at the cross, doomed to a final end. He is also still operating. Believers cannot afford to imagine him already in his final cage.

Milton's Hero

In 1667 the English poet John Milton published Paradise Lost, by most assessments the greatest epic poem in the English language. It is also the single most influential work ever written about Satan in terms of its effect on popular Christian imagination, and its influence has not been entirely healthy.

Milton's Satan is not Dante's frozen grotesque. He is portrayed as magnificent. He is proud, articulate, and defiant. He organizes the fallen angels in hell with the rhetoric of a general. He crosses the abyss between hell and earth with the courage of an explorer. He delivers soliloquies of anguished self-awareness that are among the most psychologically compelling passages in English literature. He declares: "Better to reign in Hell than serve in Heaven." Generations of readers have found that line more attractive than they expected to.

The poet William Blake famously said that Milton was "of the Devil's party without knowing it," suggesting that Milton's poetic sympathies had made Satan the moral hero of a poem designed to justify the ways of God to men. What is not debated is the effect. Milton's Satan is interesting in a way Dante's is not, compelling in a way Scripture's Adversary rarely is taken to be. He has grandeur. He has a tragic backstory. He has the features of an epic hero.

The problem is that Scripture does not present Satan this way. The roaring lion of 1 Peter 5:8 does not give compelling speeches. The father of lies in John 8:44 does not have a tragic backstory worth sympathizing with. The romantic reading of Satan produces a real-world effect. It makes the Adversary seem like someone whose perspective has merit, someone who was treated unfairly by authority and responded with admirable defiance. That reading is not theologically neutral. It is the Serpent's argument in the garden, dressed in better language.

Ask yourself this. Why is Milton's Satan attractive? Because he speaks the language of every adolescent rebellion. Authority is arbitrary. The system is unfair. The defiant rebel is the figure with integrity. Submission is for the weak. Self-determination is the highest virtue. Anyone who has been a young person knows this script. Anyone who has been a parent has heard it. The Devil did not invent it for Milton. The Devil invented it in the garden. Milton just gave it the most beautiful poetry it has ever had. And once a young reader has been moved by the poetry, the underlying argument has gotten further into us than we realize.

This is the practical reason for caution about Paradise Lost as a young Christian. The book is not evil. It is a work of genius and a serious meditation on the Fall. But the way it presents Satan is dangerous in proportion to the reader's spiritual maturity. The reader who has not yet built up a strong biblical picture of the Devil will absorb Milton's Satan as the picture, and that picture will distort our thinking for years afterward.

Why Both Distortions Serve the Adversary

The monster and the romantic hero seem like opposites. One produces repulsion. The other produces attraction. But they serve the same function for the Adversary. Both prevent a clear-eyed view of what Scripture actually describes.

Dante's monster is so hideous and powerless that it produces revulsion or dismissal. Neither prepares a believer to recognize the sophisticated, intelligent, patient Adversary that 2 Corinthians 2:11 warns about. If Satan looks like a three-headed frozen grotesque, you are not looking for him in the arguments that sound almost right, the teachers who come as angels of light, the plausible alternatives to what God has said.

Milton's romantic rebel is so attractive that it produces sympathy. And sympathy for an Adversary is not a spiritually neutral position. If pride is noble, if defiance of God is heroic, if the rebel against heaven is the one with the interesting speeches, then the fall from heaven looks like a brave act rather than the catastrophic moral failure Scripture describes it as.

The biblical picture is neither. The Adversary is real, capable, dangerous, and actively hostile. He is also a creature. Bounded. Limited. Defeated at the cross. Doomed to the lake of fire. He deserves neither the fear that makes you irrational nor the sympathy that makes you complicit. He deserves the sober, vigilant resistance that 1 Peter 5:9 describes.

The Modern Variations

The medieval and Renaissance distortions did not stay in their century. They evolved. Each generation has produced its own variations on these two basic types, monster or romantic hero, with new costumes for the cultural moment.

The horror movie Devil is the monster updated for film. He is the demonic figure in scary movies, the supernatural villain whose purpose is to terrify the audience for ninety minutes. He is the descendant of Dante's grotesque, with better special effects. He produces the same effect Dante's monster produced. Once the movie ends, the audience walks out of the theater and forgets the figure existed. He has nothing to do with their actual lives. The lesson the movie teaches, even if accidentally, is that the Devil is the kind of thing that exists only in stories.

The sympathetic Devil of streaming series and graphic novels is Milton's Satan updated for the present. He is the protagonist with a point of view, the misunderstood outsider, the witty rebel. The shows that present this Devil are usually well-made. The character is engaging. The audience is invited, episode after episode, to take the Devil's side of the argument. Some of these series have run for years and accumulated millions of viewers. The cumulative effect is a generation that has been quietly trained to see the Devil as a sympathetic figure with grievances worth hearing.

The aesthetic Devil is the social media variation. Inverted crosses, pentagrams, sigils circulated as visual style. Most users intend nothing theological. The symbols have become decoration. But the symbols still mean what they mean. The constant circulation, even as decoration, normalizes an aesthetic that is not aesthetically neutral. A young person scrolling through a thousand of these images is being slowly habituated to imagery that, only a few generations ago, would have been recognized immediately as serving a specific spiritual agenda.

The deconstructionist Devil is the philosophical variation. He is presented in essays, podcasts, and books as a symbol rather than a being. He is "what we project onto the universe to explain evil." He is "a useful metaphor for the negative aspects of human psychology." The effect of this framing is to dissolve the Devil entirely. If he is just a symbol, no one needs to resist him. If he is just psychology, the cure is therapy, not the gospel. The Devil benefits enormously from being treated as a symbol, because a symbol cannot be opposed in any meaningful way.

Each of these modern variations runs on the same machinery as the medieval distortions. Each one is a substitute for the biblical picture. Each one is doing the same work, just with updated styling.

What the Bible Says Versus What We Are Told

Think about this for a minute. The Bible spends thousands of words describing the Adversary, his methods, his hierarchy, his limits, and his defeat. Most Christians, including most adult Christians, could not give an accurate summary of what those thousands of words actually say. Why? Because most of what they think they know came from sources other than the Bible. Movies. Sermons that quoted other sermons that quoted other sermons. Folk traditions. Political rhetoric. Halloween. Cartoon imagery absorbed in childhood.

The cure is the practice this book is modeling. Read the text. Let the text say what it says. Hold the text against the cultural picture and notice the difference. Where they conflict, the text wins. Where the cultural picture has added details that are not in the text, those details have to be put down. They are not yours to keep. They were inherited from people who had their own reasons for adding them, and most of those reasons were not biblical.

This is hard work. It feels like losing something at first, because the cultural picture is vivid and familiar, and the biblical picture is leaner and stranger. But the leaner biblical picture is the true one, and the true one is the only one that gives a believer any actual help against an actual Adversary. The vivid false picture gives nothing.

The Cost of the Wrong Picture

Consider what happens when a believer goes through life with one of the false pictures dominant in our imagination. The medieval monster picture means we will not recognize the Devil when he comes wearing a suit, smiling, sounding reasonable. The Milton romantic picture means we will sympathize with the Devil when he appears in literature or media as a tragic rebel, and the sympathy will move us in directions we would not have chosen if we had seen what we were sympathizing with. The horror movie picture means we will not take the Devil seriously at all, because he belongs to the world of fiction. The aesthetic picture means we will surround ourselves with imagery that, even if it does not reach our conscious thoughts, is shaping our habits of mind. The deconstructionist picture means we will not believe the Adversary exists, which means we will not put on any armor against him.

Every one of these costs is real. None of them shows up immediately. They show up at the moment of testing, when the actual Adversary uses an actual method and the believer reaches for what we think we know about him and finds the wrong toolkit in our hands.

The Adversary loves the wrong toolkit. He helped design it.

How the False Pictures Got into the Church

It would be one thing if the false pictures of the Devil had stayed outside the church. They did not. They got in. And they got in through specific channels that are still operating.

The first channel is sermons that quote other sermons. A preacher hears a vivid description of the Devil from another preacher. He uses it in his own sermon. His listeners absorb it. Some of them go on to preach themselves and pass it along. After three or four generations of this, no one remembers where the description came from. It is just what everyone says. Some of these descriptions came from Scripture. A lot of them came from somebody's imagination, two centuries back, who had absorbed Dante or Milton or a Hieronymus Bosch painting. The image traveled. The source got lost.

The second channel is curriculum and resources designed for children. Sunday school illustrations show demons with horns. Vacation Bible School plays cast the Devil as a red figure with a tail. Christian movies for kids feature villains who look exactly like the medieval grotesque. The intentions are good. The visuals stick. By the time those children reach adulthood, they have a picture of the Devil that was never in their Bible to begin with. Their adult faith has to either work past that picture or stay limited by it.

The third channel is fiction marketed to Christians. There is a tradition of Christian novels and films that depict spiritual warfare with vivid imagery, demonic encounters with melodramatic flourishes, and a Devil whose appearance and methods owe more to the horror genre than to the text of Scripture. These works often have devout intentions. They want to make the reality of spiritual warfare vivid. The unintended consequence is that they teach a generation of believers to expect the Devil to be vivid in those particular ways, and when he comes in his actual subtler ways, they do not recognize him.

The fourth channel is the broader culture, soaking through. A Christian young person watches the same movies as our non-Christian peers. We scroll the same social media. We absorb the same ambient imagery. None of it is labeled as theological instruction. All of it is forming our imagination of what the Devil looks like. The Bible has to compete for us mental space against thousands of hours of cultural input that is going in continuously, often without anyone, including us, noticing.

The cure is not to escape the culture. The cure is to know the Bible's picture so well that the cultural picture has to compete on disadvantageous terms. The believer who has read Job 1 and Genesis 3 and 2 Corinthians 11 and Ephesians 6 carefully, multiple times, has a biblical picture of the Devil with depth and detail. Cultural input still arrives, but it cannot replace what is already there. The biblical picture has the home field.

That is what this book is trying to do. By the end, you will have a picture of the Devil built from the actual texts. The cultural images will still exist around you, but they will compete against something solid. That is the protection. That is also the offense. A believer with the biblical picture in our heads can name what is happening when we see a movie or scrolls past a meme. We can say, that is Pan with horns. That is Milton's romantic rebel. That is Dante's frozen monster. That is the deconstructionist symbol. None of those is the Devil the Bible describes. None of them is what I am dealing with.

What This Chapter Establishes

One. The popular visual image of the Devil is not from Scripture. It was assembled from Greek mythology, medieval art, and literary invention over many centuries.

Two. Dante's monster and Milton's romantic hero are the two most influential literary inventions. Both are widely carried. Both are wrong.

Three. Each wrong picture produces a specific vulnerability. The monster produces dismissal. The romantic hero produces sympathy.

Four. Modern variations of the same two types continue to work in horror films, streaming series, social media aesthetics, and academic deconstructions. The styling changes. The function does not.

Five. The biblical Adversary deserves neither dismissal nor sympathy. He deserves sober, vigilant resistance.

Hold these five. The next chapter shows that these distortions are not accidental. They align with a specific pattern the Adversary himself uses. Presenting himself attractively, as an angel of light.

Review Questions

1. Genesis 3:1 describes the Serpent as *"more subtil than any beast of the field."* What visual details does the Bible give about the Adversary in this passage, and what details does it not give?

2. The horns, cloven hooves, and goat features of the popular Devil image came from Pan, a figure in Greek and Roman mythology. How did these features migrate from pagan gods to Christian art?

3. 1 Corinthians 10:20 says that the things Gentiles sacrifice *"they sacrifice to devils, and not to God."* How did this verse shape the strategy of early Christian artists in depicting demonic beings?

4. The chapter explains the strategic reason medieval artists made pagan gods look monstrous: to undo their appeal. What was the unintended consequence of this strategy over time?

5. The pitchfork has no biblical origin. Where did it come from, and how did it become the universal symbol associated with the Devil?

6. The chapter says that the medieval image of the Devil, designed to terrify a fourteenth-century peasant, has lost its scare for a twenty-first-century young person. Why might the Devil be content with this development?

7. Dante's Satan is described as "powerless, imprisoned, self-defeating." How is this portrait more theologically honest than the popular image, and how does it fail?

8. The chapter argues that Dante's image places the Devil in his future destination rather than his current address. What is the difference, and why does it matter for believers today?

9. Milton's Satan says, "Better to reign in Hell than serve in Heaven." Why does the chapter identify this line as dangerous rather than merely dramatic?

10. William Blake said Milton was "of the Devil's party without knowing it." What did Blake mean, and what does this illustrate about the effect of the romantic hero portrayal?

11. The chapter says Milton's Satan speaks "the language of every adolescent rebellion." What is the script, and why does it matter that the Devil invented it in the garden, not Milton in 1667?

12. The chapter describes four modern variations of the false Devil: the horror movie monster, the sympathetic streaming protagonist, the social media aesthetic, and the deconstructionist symbol. How does each one work, and how does each one serve the Adversary's purposes?

13. The chapter says, "The vivid false picture gives nothing." What does it mean to say that the leaner biblical picture is the only one that gives a believer actual help?

14. The chapter concludes that the biblical Adversary *"deserves neither dismissal nor sympathy."* How does this sober posture set up the next chapter on the cultural Devil and 2 Corinthians 11:14?

REFERENCES

1. On the origin of the Devil's visual features in Greco-Roman mythology, see Jeffrey Burton Russell, Lucifer: The Devil in the Middle Ages (Ithaca: Cornell University Press, 1984).

2. On the four-volume historical study of Satan's image, see Jeffrey Burton Russell, The Devil (1977); Satan (1981); Lucifer (1984); Mephistopheles (1986); all from Cornell University Press.

3. On Dante's Satan in Canto XXXIV of the Inferno, see Robin Kirkpatrick, Dante: The Divine Comedy (New York: Cambridge University Press, 2004).

4. On Milton's Satan and the "Devil's party" debate, see C. S. Lewis, A Preface to Paradise Lost (London: Oxford University Press, 1942).

5. On the Sant'Apollinare Nuovo mosaic and the development of the red Devil image, see Russell, Lucifer.

6. On the modern entertainment industry's portrayal of Satan, see W. Scott Poole, Satan in America: The Devil We Know (Lanham: Rowman and Littlefield, 2009).

CHAPTER FIVE

The Cultural Devil

"For such are false apostles, deceitful workers, transforming themselves into the apostles of Christ. And no marvel; for Satan himself is transformed into an angel of light. Therefore it is no great thing if his ministers also be transformed as the ministers of righteousness; whose end shall be according to their works." (2 Corinthians 11:13-15)

In this text, Paul is warning the Corinthian church about false apostles who have been presenting themselves as genuine servants of Christ. His warning contains one of the most important statements in Scripture about how the Adversary actually presents himself. Satan transforms himself into an angel of light. Not into a monster. Not into an obvious villain. Into something that looks like what is good, trustworthy, enlightened, and sent from God.

The previous chapter detailed how the popular picture of the Devil was assembled from sources outside Scripture. This chapter builds on that observation by asking why the false pictures are so effective, and why they persist. The answer is that the distortions are not accidental. They align with a specific strategy the Adversary himself uses. The cultural pictures of Satan succeed, in part, because they correspond to how he actually operates. By disguise.

Notice the precision of Paul's language. He does not say Satan occasionally pretends. He does not say Satan sometimes uses a cover. He says Satan is transformed into an angel of light. The verb is the same root used in Matthew 17:2 to describe the transfiguration of Christ. It is the language of total transformation, full disguise, an appearance that fully conceals what is underneath. This is not a costume. It is a counterfeit identity, sustained from the inside.

The Disguise Is the Primary Mode

Paul does not say Satan occasionally pretends to be attractive. He says Satan is transformed into an angel of light. The verb is the same root used for describing the transfiguration of Christ in Matthew 17:2. Paul is using strong language to make a clear point. Attractive presentation is not an occasional tactic but the Adversary's primary mode of operation.

This shapes how a person should think about temptation, deception, and cultural influence. The most dangerous version of the Adversary is not the one that announces what he is. It is the one that looks like something worth respecting, something enlightened, something sophisticated. Paul continues in verse 15: "*it is no great thing if his ministers also be transformed as the ministers of righteousness.*" The disguise runs through every level of the work.

The Genesis 3 encounter is the template, and Chapter Six will work through it in detail. The Serpent did not come as a monster. He came as a reasonable voice asking a reasonable question. He did not tell Eve that God was evil. He suggested that God's command might be more restrictive than necessary. Every attractive presentation of the Adversary since has followed this pattern. He does not argue for evil. He argues for a more enlightened good.

This is also why discernment is one of the most important spiritual skills a young Christian can develop. Discernment is the ability to recognize what something actually is when its surface appearance is designed to hide what it actually is. Hebrews 5:14 says discernment belongs to those who, "*by reason of use have their senses exercised to discern both good and evil.*" The senses get exercised by being used. Discernment is not given as a gift on a single occasion. It is developed by a lifetime of paying close attention to what Scripture says, and comparing what shows up in the world with what Scripture says, and noticing the gaps.

The Monster and the Angel of Light

The previous chapter described the two literary distortions of the Adversary. The monstrous Dante figure and the romantic Milton figure. This chapter can now name why both endure.

The monstrous figure endures because it is vivid and produces a strong reaction. But the reaction is the wrong one. It produces dismissal. A believer who has processed the Adversary mainly through monster imagery will not recognize him when he appears as an angel of light. The monster trains the eye to look for the obvious. The angel of light is not obvious. That is precisely the point.

The romantic figure endures because it resembles what 2 Corinthians 11:14 actually describes. Milton's Satan is attractive, articulate, and articulate in a way that sounds enlightened. Readers have sympathized with him for over three centuries. That sympathy, extended to a literary character, is not spiritually neutral because the character is an accurate likeness of how Scripture says the Adversary presents himself. Sympathy for the disguise is the disguise working.

Between the two, the romantic figure is the more dangerous. The monster is obviously wrong. Most people will not adopt him as a role model. But the charming rebel who raises thoughtful questions about divine authority is a version of something Scripture directly warns about. The believer who finds Milton's Satan more compelling than we expected is, at some level, being recruited into his argument.

There is a way to test this in your own life. Ask whether the artistic or cultural representations of the Devil that have most moved you, the ones that have stayed with you, the ones that have made him seem interesting or sympathetic, are functioning as actual training in how to think about him. Then ask whether that training has been making you more or less ready to recognize the actual Devil when he shows up. The honest answer is usually less. The romantic Devil is so attractive precisely because he is doing the work of the actual Devil with much better marketing.

The Cultural Patterns That Follow

Because the attractive disguise is the Adversary's primary mode, and because cultural imagination has picked up on this disguise through Milton and his inheritors, a predictable pattern appears across media and literature. The Adversary is presented as one of four figures.

The Rebel

A rebel against arbitrary authority. The suggestion is that divine authority is arbitrary, that rebellion is principled, and that the rebel is the figure with integrity. Milton's "Better to reign in Hell than serve in Heaven" establishes this template. The rebel-Devil shows up in books, films, songs, and poetry as a heroic resister of God's tyranny. The framing assumes God's authority needs to be resisted. The framing is the lie. God's authority is not arbitrary. It is the authority of a perfect Creator over His creation. Rebellion against perfect authority is not heroic. It is suicidal. But the framing makes it look heroic, and the heroic framing makes the lie effective.

The Questioner

A sophisticated questioner of simple belief. The suggestion is that the religious are naive and the Devil's perspective is more enlightened. This is the Serpent in Genesis 3, asking "*Hath God said*?" in a way that makes the question sound like intellectual honesty. The sophisticated-Devil shows up in academic writing, on podcasts, in essays, in college dorm conversations. He is presented as the figure who is willing to ask the hard questions that timid believers refuse to ask. The framing is again the lie. The hardest questions any believer will ever ask are not the ones the Devil suggests. They are the questions God Himself has answered in Scripture and asks His people to wrestle with there. The Devil's questions are not bold. They are the same questions he has been asking since Eden.

The Sympathizer

A sympathetic outsider. The suggestion is that the Adversary has been misunderstood, treated unfairly, and deserves a hearing. The twenty-first-century versions of this pattern appear in streaming series, graphic novels, and films that present Satan as a protagonist with understandable grievances. He is the witty bachelor who runs a bar in Los Angeles. He is the misunderstood prince who just wants the throne his father took from him. He is the sad fallen angel who would maybe come back if anyone would just listen to him. Every one of these stories runs the same scam. They make the Devil sympathetic by giving him a backstory the Bible does not give him. They invite the audience to feel for him. The feeling, once invited, is real, and it does real spiritual work.

The Aesthetic

A stylistic aesthetic. Inverted crosses, pentagrams, occult imagery circulate as visual style on social media, detached from any specific belief content. Most who use them intend nothing theological. But the symbols have real referents, and the constant circulation normalizes an aesthetic that is not aesthetically neutral. A young person scrolling past a thousand of these images is being formed by them, even when we are not consciously thinking about them. The repetition is the point. Symbols become familiar. Familiar things become acceptable. Acceptable things stop registering as warning signs. The aesthetic-Devil is the most subtle of the four because it works on the visual habit, not on the conscious reasoning.

Each of these patterns corresponds to the angel-of-light disguise. Each presents the Adversary as a more interesting, more enlightened, more sympathetic figure than the pedestrian world of ordinary obedience to God.

The Strategy in Real Time

What these patterns add up to, taken together, is a coordinated cultural project. Not coordinated by the artists themselves. Most of them are sincere and not consciously serving any spiritual agenda. But coordinated by the Adversary, who has been working through human culture for as long as human culture has existed.

He uses what is available. In a medieval Christian society, he had the church itself to work through, getting cultural distortions of his image into stained glass and homilies. In a Renaissance and Reformation society, he had the printing press, getting Milton's Paradise Lost in front of millions of readers across centuries. In a twentieth-century society, he had film, getting horror movies and romantic-Devil dramas in front of audiences in the dark. In a twenty-first-century society, he has streaming services, social media, video games, podcasts, and the algorithmic feed that delivers his preferred image of himself directly into a young person's hand a hundred times a day.

He does not need each individual artist to be conscious of what is happening. He just needs the cumulative effect. Over a lifetime, the cumulative effect on a young person is enormous. By the time we are twenty-five, we have absorbed, without ever choosing to, thousands of hours of content shaped by the romantic-Devil framing or the sympathetic-Devil framing or the aesthetic-Devil framing. Most of that content was made by people who would not describe themselves as serving the Devil. The Devil does not care. The work got done.

This is also why simple cultural withdrawal is not the answer. The believer cannot wall ourselves off from the culture and expect to be safe. The patterns are too pervasive. They will reach us through people we trust, through media we consume for entertainment, through conversations we have with friends. The only protection is a mind so saturated with the actual biblical picture that the cultural picture cannot displace it. Romans 12:2 will say it directly in a moment.

Colossians 2:8 and the Capture of the Mind

> *"Beware lest any man spoil you through philosophy and vain deceit, after the tradition of men, after the rudiments of the world, and not after Christ."* (Colossians 2:8)

The Greek word translated "spoil" is *sulagogeo*, meaning to carry off as plunder, to take captive. Paul is not warning against thinking. He is warning against the capture of the mind by frameworks organized around a center other than Christ.

A person who has been shaped by the cultural portraits of the Adversary has had our imagination formed, to some degree, by images and associations that are not rooted in the text. The believer who cannot think about the Adversary without first passing through the visual vocabulary of Dante, the psychological vocabulary of Milton, or the aesthetic vocabulary of contemporary media is working against our own discernment.

Romans 12:2 gives the remedy:

> *"And be not conformed to this world: but be ye transformed by the renewing of your mind, that ye may prove what is that good, and acceptable, and perfect, will of God."*

The mind has to be actively re-formed by the Word of God, because the passive process of cultural formation has been working on it since you were old enough to take in a story.

The practical question is not whether you have been influenced by cultural portraits of the Adversary. You have. The question is whether you will do the work of reading what Scripture actually says and allowing that reading to displace what the culture has put there.

How does that work in practice? It works through repetition. Read the actual passages of Scripture about the Devil over and over. Genesis 3. Job 1 and 2. Zechariah 3. Matthew 4. Luke 10. Ephesians 6. 1 Peter 5. Revelation 12. These passages contain the picture. The more you read them, the more they shape what you see when you think about the Devil. After enough repetition, when you encounter a cultural representation of the Devil, you can compare it to the biblical picture immediately. You will notice what is wrong about it before you have absorbed any of it.

Repetition is not glamorous. It is the same passages, again and again, slowly forming the imagination until the biblical picture is the default. There is no shortcut for this work. There is also no substitute. The believer who skips this work and tries to operate on a vague cultural picture of the Devil will be working against ourselves for the rest of our lives.

What Discernment Looks Like

Discernment is the practical fruit of having a biblical picture rooted deeply in the mind. Here is what it looks like in real situations.

A young Christian encounters a teacher who is sophisticated, articulate, and presents their version of Christianity in a fresh way that everyone in our circle is excited about. We listen carefully. We compare what he is saying to Scripture. We notice that some of what he is saying departs from what Scripture says. The departure is not loud. It is subtle. He is not denying any major doctrine. He is just adjusting things slightly. But the adjustments add up. We decide not to follow him, not because we are closed-minded, but because we have noticed the gaps. That is discernment.

A young Christian is invited to listen to a podcast that is presenting "the other side" of various biblical issues. We listen to one episode. The hosts are smart and seem fair-minded. The framing is "let's just ask the questions." But we notice that the questions are all asked in one direction. The doubts run only one way. The conclusions, when they come, all land on the side that loosens the authority of Scripture. We stop listening, not because we are afraid of questions, but because we have noticed the pattern. That is discernment.

A young Christian sees a movie everyone is talking about. The villain is the most interesting character in the film. The villain's argument is the one the audience is invited to find compelling. We notice what is happening as we watch. We enjoy the craft of the movie. We do not adopt the villain's argument as our own. We separate the artistry from the message. That is discernment.

These are not extraordinary acts of spiritual perception. They are ordinary acts of someone whose mind has been formed by Scripture so that the formation does its work automatically. The believer does not have to think hard to do them. We do them because we have been built to do them. Romans 12:2 has happened in our lives. The mind has been renewed. The renewal is paying off.

When the Disguise Slips

There are moments when the disguise of the Adversary slips, even briefly, and Scripture records what happens then. These moments are useful because they show what is underneath when the angel-of-light masquerade comes off.

Acts 13 has one such moment. Paul and Barnabas are on Cyprus, and they encounter a sorcerer named Bar-jesus, also called Elymas. He is the religious advisor of the Roman proconsul Sergius Paulus, and when the gospel comes through Paul, Elymas tries to keep Sergius Paulus from believing. Look at what Paul says to him under the inspiration of the Holy Spirit:

> *"O full of all subtilty and all mischief, thou child of the devil, thou enemy of all righteousness, wilt thou not cease to pervert the right ways of the Lord?"* (Acts 13:10)

Paul clearly points out what is happening underneath the religious facade. The sorcerer presented himself as a wise advisor. He was actually a child of the Devil opposing the gospel. The disguise slipped because Paul, by the Spirit, called it what it was. Elymas was struck blind for a season, and Sergius Paulus believed.

Notice the pattern. The disguise was holding until someone with discernment named what was actually under it. The naming did not reveal anything Elymas himself did not know. It revealed what others around him had been unable to see. That is one of the practical functions of biblical discernment. The believer who can name what is actually happening helps everyone else around us see it too.

Another moment is in 1 Kings 22, in the story of the prophet Micaiah. King Ahab gathers four hundred prophets who all tell him to go to battle and win. One man, Micaiah, says the opposite. When pressed, Micaiah describes what he has been shown: a lying spirit was permitted, by God, to go forth and entice Ahab through the mouths of the four hundred prophets. The four hundred were sincere. They thought they were prophesying truly. They were operating under a spirit they did not know was lying. Micaiah's gift was the ability to see what was actually moving them. The disguise slipped because a man with the Spirit of God could see past it.

These moments are not common. Most of the time the disguise holds. But the moments when it slips are valuable because they remind a believer that the disguise is real, that it is operating constantly, and that biblical discernment is what cuts through it.

The Modern Equivalents

Look at the angel-of-light pattern in modern Christian life. It does not announce itself. It comes in forms that look like enlightenment, like progress, like maturity, like compassion. Each of these has a true version that is good, and a counterfeit version that the Adversary uses. Telling them apart is the work of discernment.

Enlightenment in its true form means the renewing of the mind by Scripture, which makes a believer more able to see God's purposes and to live in alignment with them. Enlightenment in its counterfeit form is the suggestion that the believer needs to move past the simple, plain meaning of Scripture into a more sophisticated reading that, conveniently, ends up agreeing with the surrounding culture. The counterfeit feels more enlightened. It is actually a return to the Serpent's first question.

Progress in its true form means growth in Christ-likeness, in love, in obedience, in holiness. Progress in its counterfeit form is the suggestion that the church needs to move past its old positions on whatever the culture is currently impatient with. The counterfeit feels like progress. It is actually a step away from the unchanging Word of God.

Maturity in its true form means the steady deepening of faith and the steady maturation of judgment that comes from years of walking with Christ. Maturity in its counterfeit form is the cynical posture of someone who has seen through the simple faith of younger believers and now holds a more nuanced view, which usually means a less obedient view. The counterfeit feels mature. It is actually a hardening that the Bible warns against.

Compassion in its true form means the love of God flowing through a believer toward those who are hurting, lost, or in need. Compassion in its counterfeit form is the suggestion that real love means not telling people the truth about sin and judgment, because that would hurt them. The counterfeit feels compassionate. It is actually the cruelest thing a believer can do, because it withholds the only thing that can save the person being loved.

In each case, the true and the counterfeit look similar on the surface. That is the whole point. The Adversary does not bother counterfeiting things that have no value. He counterfeits the things that look most like real Christian virtue, because those are the disguises that work best. The believer who has not learned to tell the difference between the true and the counterfeit version of each of these will be moved, slowly and steadily, away from Christ while believing we are moving closer to Him.

This is why every chapter of this book has insisted on going back to what Scripture actually says. There is no other way to tell the true from the counterfeit. The believer who has not built our sense of true Christian virtue from the actual text of Scripture will inevitably take our sense of it from the surrounding culture. And the surrounding culture is exactly the place the Adversary has been working to install the counterfeits.

What This Chapter Establishes

One. Satan's primary mode of presentation is disguise. 2 Corinthians 11:14 names it directly.

Two. The monster and the romantic hero both serve the Adversary because each one corresponds, in different ways, to how he actually operates.

Three. Cultural patterns of presenting Satan, in every medium, tend to follow the angel-of-light template. Rebel, sophisticate, outsider, aesthetic.

Four. The cultural project is coordinated by the Adversary working through whatever media are available in any given era. The cumulative effect on a young person is enormous.

Five. The remedy is not cultural withdrawal but the active renewing of the mind by Scripture. What the culture has formed, the Word must reform.

Six. Discernment is the practical fruit of a mind formed by Scripture. It looks like ordinary judgment in real situations, but it requires Scripture to have done its work first.

Hold these six. The next chapter takes up the specific method the Adversary uses on a human being. 2 Corinthians 11:14 tells us the disguise. Genesis 3 shows us the sequence.

Review Questions

1. 2 Corinthians 11:13-15 describes false apostles as *"ministers of righteousness"* whose ultimate source is the Adversary. What does this passage establish about the primary mode of Satan's presentation?

2. Paul says Satan "is transformed into an angel of light," not that he occasionally pretends to be attractive. What is the difference between an occasional tactic and a primary mode of operation?

3. Hebrews 5:14 says discernment belongs to those who *"by reason of use have their senses exercised to discern both good and evil."* How does this verse describe the way discernment is developed?

4. The chapter argues that the romantic hero portrayal of Satan (Milton) is more dangerous than the monster portrayal (Dante). Why?

5. The Serpent in Genesis 3 did not come as a monster. He came as a reasonable voice. How does this pattern correspond to 2 Corinthians 11:14?

6. The chapter identifies four recurring cultural patterns in the presentation of Satan: the rebel, the sophisticate, the sympathetic outsider, and the aesthetic style. How does each one correspond to the angel-of-light disguise?

7. The chapter argues that the cultural project of the Devil is "coordinated" without each individual artist being conscious of what is happening. What does this mean, and what does it imply for how a believer evaluates art and media?

8. The inverted cross, pentagram, and occult imagery circulate on social media as stylistic content, often without any specific belief attached. Why does the chapter argue this pattern still matters?

9. Colossians 2:8 warns against being *"spoiled"* (*sulagogeo*, carried off as plunder) by frameworks *"not after Christ."* How does this verse apply to the cultural formation of the imagination discussed in this chapter?

10. Romans 12:2 tells believers to be *"transformed by the renewing of your mind."* Why is active mental re-formation necessary in the face of cultural portraits of the Adversary, and how does the chapter say this works in practice?

11. The chapter says simple cultural withdrawal is not the answer. Why not, and what is the alternative?

12. The chapter describes three examples of discernment in action: evaluating a teacher, evaluating a podcast, evaluating a movie. What is common to all three, and what does it tell us about how discernment actually works in real life?

13. The chapter says sympathy for Milton's Satan is sympathy for the disguise working. What does this mean for how a believer should read or engage with literary and media portrayals of the Adversary?

14. The chapter closes by saying 2 Corinthians 11:14 tells us the disguise, and Genesis 3 shows us the sequence. What is the connection between these two passages, and how does it set up Chapter Six?

REFERENCES

1. On 2 Corinthians 11:14 and the angel of light motif, see Philip Edgcumbe Hughes, Paul's Second Epistle to the Corinthians, New International Commentary on the New Testament (Grand Rapids: Eerdmans, 1962).

2. On Colossians 2:8 and the meaning of *sulagogeo*, see Peter T. O'Brien, The Letter to the Colossians and to Philemon, New International Greek Testament Commentary (Grand Rapids: Eerdmans, 1982).

3. On Romans 12:2 and the renewal of the mind, see Douglas J. Moo, The Epistle to the Romans, New International Commentary on the New Testament (Grand Rapids: Eerdmans, 1996).

4. On Hebrews 5:14 and the development of discernment, see Philip Edgcumbe Hughes, A Commentary on the Epistle to the Hebrews (Grand Rapids: Eerdmans, 1977).

5. On the cultural circulation of Satanic imagery as aesthetic, see Jesper Aagaard Petersen, ed., Contemporary Religious Satanism: A Critical Anthology (Farnham: Ashgate, 2009).

6. On the historical relationship between Christian theology and popular media depictions of evil, see W. Scott Poole, Satan in America: The Devil We Know (Lanham: Rowman and Littlefield, 2009).

CHAPTER SIX

The Serpent's Strategy

"Now the serpent was more subtil than any beast of the field which the LORD God had made. And he said unto the woman, Yea, hath God said, Ye shall not eat of every tree of the garden? And the woman said unto the serpent, We may eat of the fruit of the trees of the garden: But of the fruit of the tree which is in the midst of the garden, God hath said, Ye shall not eat of it, neither shall ye touch it, lest ye die. And the serpent said unto the woman, Ye shall not surely die: For God doth know that in the day ye eat thereof, then your eyes shall be opened, and ye shall be as gods, knowing good and evil. And when the woman saw that the tree was good for food, and that it was pleasant to the eyes, and a tree to be desired to make one wise, she took of the fruit thereof, and did eat, and gave also unto her husband with her; and he did eat." (Genesis 3:1-6)

These six verses from Genesis chapter 3 are the most detailed account in Scripture of how the Adversary actually operates on a human person. It is not a summary. Not an abstraction. A transcript. Every temptation every human being will ever face follows the pattern laid out in this encounter, because the Adversary is still running the same strategy he ran in the garden.

The previous chapter established that Satan's primary mode is disguise, the angel of light. This chapter takes the next step. Given that he approaches by disguise, what is his actual method once he has your attention? The answer is a three-move sequence. Question the word. Deny the consequence. Offer a distorted good. Each move prepares the next. Together they form a strategy effective enough that it has been used on every human being who has ever lived.

The Hebrew word translated *"subtil"* is *arum*, meaning crafty, shrewd, or clever. It is the same root used in Proverbs 12:16 and 13:16 to describe a prudent person who thinks before acting. The word is not inherently negative. What makes the Serpent's *arum* destructive is that it is in the service of a lie. He is the most capable creature in the created order, directing that capability toward deception.

A young believer reading this chapter should put a marker in our minds right at the start. The Serpent's strategy is the same strategy you will face. Not a similar strategy. The same strategy. The Adversary does not innovate much. He has been using these three moves since the garden because they work. The specifics will vary. The cultural packaging will vary. The voice will sometimes be a friend, sometimes a teacher, sometimes a song, sometimes the inside of your own head at three in the morning. The voice changes. The script does not. Learn the script and you will recognize the voice every time.

Move One: Question the Word

> *"And he said unto the woman, Yea, hath God said, Ye shall not eat of every tree of the garden?"* (Genesis 3:1)

The first move is not an accusation. It is just a question. And the question does not attack God directly. It raises a possibility. Perhaps God's command was more restrictive than you understood it to be. Perhaps the prohibition was broader than intended. Perhaps what God said deserves to be re-examined.

Look at the subtlety of this opening. Satan does not say "God is wrong." He asks "Did God really say?" He introduces doubt as a reasonable intellectual exercise. He frames uncertainty about the Word as honest inquiry. And notice that his version of the command is slightly off. He asks about *"every tree of the garden"* when God had prohibited only one. This small distortion primes Eve to correct him, which moves her into the posture of explaining God's command rather than simply trusting in it.

This first move is immediately recognizable in current experience. The contemporary version sounds like, "Are you sure that's what the Bible actually means? Scholars disagree about this passage. Maybe that command was culturally specific. Maybe God's intent was more nuanced than a surface reading suggests." None of these questions is necessarily evil. Some of them are valid interpretive questions. But the effect, when they arrive at the wrong moment and in the wrong spirit, is exactly what the effect was in the garden. The believer's certainty about what God said is loosened.

2 Timothy 2:15 instructs the believer to *"rightly divid[e] the word of truth"* precisely because the word can be wrongly divided, subtly questioned, gently redirected. The first move in the Adversary's strategy is always an attack on the Word.

Notice something else about the first move. It places Eve in a position of authority over the Word. By asking her what God said, the Serpent invites her to summarize, interpret, and explain it. The moment she begins explaining, Eve is operating as the judge of the Word rather than the receiver of it. Even when her explanation is mostly accurate, the posture has shifted. She is no longer simply standing under the command. She is now standing over it, evaluating it. That same shift is what happens to us whenever we step into the posture of evaluating what God has said rather than receiving it. From that posture, the next moves work much more easily. The Serpent has not denied anything yet. He has just changed our relationship to the text.

This is exactly how the first move works in modern Christian experience. A Christian is asked, "What do you think about that verse?" or "How do you interpret what the Bible says about this?" The questions sound innocent. They invite reflection. But they also invite the believer to step out of the posture of receiving the Word and into the posture of evaluating it. And once we are evaluating, the door is open for the next move. The way to refuse this trap is not to refuse questions, because questions are good. The way to refuse the trap is to remain under the Word even while answering questions. To say, "Here is what God says. I receive that. Now let me think about it from there." The order matters. Submission to the Word first. Reflection second. The Serpent reverses the order. The believer should not.

Move Two: Contradict the Consequence

> *"And the serpent said unto the woman, Ye shall not surely die."* (Genesis 3:4)

The Adversary now attacks the consequence directly. God had said the day they ate from that tree they would die (Genesis 2:17). Satan contradicts the statement flatly. *"Ye shall not surely die."* This is not a nuanced reinterpretation. It is a denial of the Word of God.

But notice how the denial has been prepared. The question in verse 1 loosened Eve's grip on the certainty of the command. The doubt introduced, perhaps God said something slightly different, perhaps the prohibition was not as clear as they thought, created psychological space for the denial to land. A person completely certain of what God said cannot be moved by a flat contradiction. A person led into a posture of questioning is far more vulnerable.

The theological name for this move is *the denial of divine judgment.* The Adversary suggests that the consequences God announced will not follow the actions God prohibited. This is one of the most pervasive forms of deception operating today. People are told, by a thousand voices in a thousand contexts, that the behaviors God has identified as destructive will not produce the destruction He described. Proverbs 14:12 names the pattern exactly: *"There is a way which seemeth right unto a man, but the end thereof are the ways of death."* The way seems right because someone has told you the consequences will not follow.

Look at how the second move plays out in people's lives. The voices around them say things like, "Nothing bad will happen if you do this. Other people do it all the time and they're fine. The old rules don't apply anymore. You're being too rigid. Your parents were lied to about this. The science has changed. The culture has changed. God doesn't punish people for that anymore." Every one of these is the second move. Every one of them is an attempt to break the connection between the action God forbade and the destruction God said would follow. And the destruction follows anyway, because the connection is not arbitrary. God did not make up rules to be cruel. He named consequences that are built into the structure of His creation. The Serpent's denial does not change the structure. It just persuades people to walk into it.

Notice also that the Serpent's denial is technically partially true in a narrow sense. Adam and Eve did not die physically the moment they ate. They died spiritually that day. They began the long process of physical decay that day. They were exiled from the garden that day. Death came to them in stages. So the Serpent could later claim he had not technically lied. They had not dropped dead in the moment. But the death God had named was real and arrived on schedule. This is one of the Adversary's signature techniques. He uses the narrowest possible reading of God's words to claim he was telling the truth, when he was actually denying the substance of what God said. The narrow technicality is part of the lie. Do not be fooled by it.

Move Three: Offer a Distorted Good

> *"For God doth know that in the day ye eat thereof, then your eyes shall be opened, and ye shall be as gods, knowing good and evil."* (Genesis 3:5)

The third move is the offer. It is the most sophisticated of the three. The Adversary does not offer something obviously bad. He offers something that contains real elements of what is good. Wisdom. Open eyes. Knowledge. Likeness to God.

These are genuine goods. The desire for wisdom is not sinful. The desire to know God more fully is not sinful.

The distortion is in the path. The offer implies that God has withheld something genuinely beneficial, and that the route around His prohibition leads to that good. This is the inversion of God's character. The One who had provided a whole garden of good things, who had placed the human beings in the most privileged position in creation, who had built every genuine good into the fabric of the world He made, is now being portrayed as holding something back.

James 1:17 is the direct answer to this characterization:

> *"Every good gift and every perfect gift is from above, and cometh down from the Father of lights, with whom is no variableness, neither shadow of turning."*

The Father does not withhold good from His children. The Adversary's offer of a distorted good depends entirely on the premise that God is holding something back. That premise is false. But once the word has been questioned and the consequence denied, the false premise becomes plausible.

The three moves are now visible as a single sequence. Question what God said. Deny that the consequence will follow. Offer a distorted good that seems to deliver what the prohibition withheld. Every temptation you will ever face will follow some version of this sequence. Sometimes all three moves are explicit. Sometimes two of them have been completed by the culture before you were born, and only the third shows up in your situation. But the sequence is constant.

Look closely at what the Serpent is actually offering Eve. Likeness to God. That is the highest good a creature can want. It is also a good God Himself wants to give. Genesis 1:26 says human beings were made in the image of God. Romans 8:29 says believers are being conformed to the image of His Son. The desire to be like God is not the problem. The problem is the path. God's path to likeness with Him is through obedience and trust. The Serpent's path is through autonomy and rebellion. Same destination promised. Different roads. One road leads to where it says it leads. The other leads to ruin.

This is why the third move is so dangerous. It gets the desire right. The believer is correct to want what is being offered, in some form. The problem is the route. The route is what the Serpent supplies, and the route is the lie. Recognizing this requires the believer to think clearly about not just what we want but how we are being told to get it. A young person being offered something good through a forbidden route should ask, "Is there a way to get this through obedience to God instead?" The answer is almost always yes. God is not in the business of withholding good things. He is in the business of providing the right path to them.

The Pattern Appears Throughout Scripture

The three-move sequence is not unique to Genesis 3. It appears in recognizable form throughout Scripture wherever the Adversary is at work.

In Matthew 4, when Satan tempts Jesus in the wilderness, all three moves appear. The first temptation invites Jesus to use His power to address a genuine need, implying that the Father's provision is inadequate. The second offers genuine global authority through an illegitimate route. The third invites a test that would require God to protect Him in a situation He should not have entered, implying that the Father's care has limits that dramatic displays can overcome. Jesus refuses each by returning to the Word of God. The moves are the same. The response is different.

Look at how Jesus responds to each temptation. He does not reason with Satan. He does not engage the logic of the temptation. He does not negotiate. He says, "It is written," and quotes Scripture. Three times. That is the model for resisting the three-move sequence. Not a clever response. Not an emotional response. Not a self-confident response. The Word of God, applied directly to the specific situation. Chapter Twelve will return to this when discussing the sword of the Spirit.

John identifies the three categories in 1 John 2:16:

> *"For all that is in the world, the lust of the flesh, and the lust of the eyes, and the pride of life, is not of the Father, but is of the world."*

These correspond directly to the three temptation moves. The lust of the flesh corresponds to the offer of something that satisfies physical desire (the fruit was *"good for food"*). The lust of the eyes corresponds to something desirable to look at and to have (*"pleasant to the eyes"*). The pride of life corresponds to the aspiration to autonomous knowledge and status (*"to make one wise," "ye shall be as gods"*). The three categories are the three moves, described from inside the human person being tempted.

Look at what John is doing with this list. He is naming three doors through which every temptation enters. Every one. Lust of the flesh covers all temptations toward physical indulgence. Lust of the eyes covers all temptations toward what attracts the senses, especially toward what someone else has. Pride of life covers all temptations toward self-exaltation, toward being more than the creature you actually are. If a young Christian commits John's three categories to memory, we have a diagnostic tool that works on every temptation we will ever face. We can name which door it is coming through. Naming it is the first step toward shutting it.

David and Bathsheba, in 2 Samuel 11, run the sequence in reverse. The lust of the eyes (David sees Bathsheba bathing). The lust of the flesh (David sends for her and lies with her). The pride of life (David tries to cover the sin with manipulation and finally murder, treating himself as above the consequences God has named for adultery and homicide). All three doors. The whole story compressed into one chapter. And David, who was the man after God's own heart, ran the same script the Serpent ran on Eve, just in a different order.

This is one of the more sobering observations in the Old Testament. Even David, even the man after God's own heart, even the king of Israel anointed by Samuel, was vulnerable to the same three moves the Serpent used in the garden. There is no spiritual maturity that immunizes a Christian against the sequence. There is only ongoing vigilance, ongoing dependence on the Word of God, and ongoing resistance from a posture of submission to God. The Christian who thinks we have outgrown the need for these things is the believer most likely to repeat David's mistake.

James 1:14-15: The Mechanism Inside the Person

> *"But every man is tempted, when he is drawn away of his own lust, and enticed. Then when lust hath conceived, it hath brought forth sin: and sin, when it is finished, bringeth forth death."* (James 1:14-15)

James places the mechanism of temptation partly inside the person being tempted, not only in the external Adversary. The Adversary offers the distorted good. But it registers as attractive because something in the person finds it attractive. Eve was not forced. She saw that the tree was good for food, pleasant to the eyes, and desired to make wise, and she took.

This detail is uncomfortable because it points in two directions at once. Toward the Adversary who constructed the offer, and toward the human person who found it compelling. Both are true at the same time. The Adversary is real and responsible for the deception. The person is also real and responsible for the choice. These two truths do not cancel each other. Blaming the Serpent entirely, as Eve did in Genesis 3:13, does not eliminate her responsibility. Focusing only on the internal inclination does not eliminate the Adversary's role.

Understanding the Serpent's strategy does not make a believer immune to it. It does mean a believer can recognize the moves as they are being made. The question that subtly undermines confidence in what God said. The voice that gently suggests the consequences will not follow. The offer that presents a genuine good through a forbidden route. These are not random pressures from a chaotic universe. They are a strategy that has been running continuously since the garden.

1 Corinthians 10:13 is the promise that applies here:

> *"There hath no temptation taken you but such as is common to man: but God is faithful, who will not suffer you to be tempted above that ye are able; but will with the temptation also make a way to escape, that ye may be able to bear it."*

Look at the four things this verse promises. First, no temptation that comes to you is unique. It has come to many people before you and they have made it through. Second, God is faithful, which is the foundation under everything else in the verse. Third, you will not be tempted above what you are able. The Adversary cannot exceed the limits God has placed on him in your specific case. Fourth, with every temptation God provides a way to escape. There is always a door out. The Adversary likes you to believe there is no door out, that you have been backed into a corner, that the only way through is to give in. That is a lie. There is always a door, and God has put it there, and your job is to look for it instead of looking at the temptation.

The Three Moves and the Three Defenses

If the Adversary uses three moves, the believer's defense should be organized accordingly. There are three corresponding defenses, each of them rooted in Scripture and each of them practical enough for a young Christian to use.

Against the first move, the defense is rootedness in the Word. The Adversary cannot question what God said to a believer who knows what God said. The question, "Did God really say?" loses its force the moment the believer answers, "Yes, He did, and here is the verse." Memorization of Scripture is not a Sunday school skill. It is armor for a real war. The verses you know by heart are the ones available to you in the moment of temptation. The verses you have only heard about are not.

Against the second move, the defense is trust in God's character. The Adversary's denial of consequence works only if the believer doubts whether God means what He says. A believer who has spent time meditating on God's faithfulness, on the consistency of His Word across centuries, is not easily moved by, "Nothing will happen. The rules don't apply. God doesn't really mind." We know better, because we know God better.

Against the third move, the defense is contentment in what God has given. The Adversary's offer of a distorted good works only if the believer feels we are missing something God has withheld. A believer who has cultivated thankfulness for what God has given, who has learned to see our own life as full of the kindness of God, is not easily seduced by the suggestion that God is holding something back. We know He is not. We have the evidence in our own life.

Three moves. Three defenses. The Word, God's character, and contentment. Each one strengthens the others. Together they form a wall that the Serpent's strategy is not designed to climb.

What This Chapter Establishes

One. The Adversary uses a consistent three-move strategy. Question the word. Deny the consequence. Offer a distorted good.

Two. The strategy is visible most clearly in Genesis 3 but appears throughout Scripture, including in the wilderness temptation of Jesus, in the categories of 1 John 2:16, and in the sin of David in 2 Samuel 11.

Three. The strategy works because each move prepares the next. Doubt enables denial. Denial enables acceptance of the distorted good.

Four. The mechanism of temptation involves both the external Adversary and an internal inclination in the person being tempted. Both are real. Both matter.

Five. The defense is built around three corresponding strengths. Rootedness in the Word, trust in God's character, and contentment in what God has given.

Review Questions

1. Genesis 3:1 says the Serpent was *"more subtil than any beast of the field."* The Hebrew word *arum* means crafty, shrewd, or clever. What does this word tell us about how the Adversary approaches temptation?

2. The first move in Genesis 3 is a question: "Hath God said?" Why is a question more effective as an opening than a direct accusation?

3. The Serpent's version of God's command in Genesis 3:1 is slightly wrong. He asks about *"every tree"* when God had prohibited only one. What is the strategic purpose of this small distortion?

4. The chapter says the first move shifts Eve from being "the receiver of" the Word to being "the judge of" the Word. How does this posture change everything that comes after it?

5. The second move is the flat denial: "Ye shall not surely die." How did the first move prepare the ground for the second move to be effective?

6. The chapter notes that the Serpent's denial was technically partially true in a narrow sense, since Adam and Eve did not drop dead the moment they ate. How does this relate to the Adversary's signature use of narrow technicalities?

7. The third move offers something that contains real elements of genuine good. Why is an offer of distorted good more dangerous than an offer of something obviously bad?

8. The Serpent's offer was likeness to God, which is in fact what God Himself wants to give His people (Romans 8:29). What is the difference between God's path to that likeness and the Serpent's?

9. James 1:17 says *"Every good gift and every perfect gift is from above."* How does this verse answer the premise on which the Adversary's offer depends?

10. The three-move pattern appears in the wilderness temptation in Matthew 4. How does Jesus's response in each case model what resistance looks like?

11. 1 John 2:16 identifies *"the lust of the flesh, and the lust of the eyes, and the pride of life."* How do these three categories correspond to the three moves in Genesis 3?

12. The chapter cites 2 Samuel 11 as showing David running the same three doors. What does it mean that even the man after God's own heart was vulnerable to the Serpent's strategy?

13. James 1:14-15 places the mechanism of temptation partly inside the person being tempted. How does this change the way we understand our own responsibility in temptation?

14. 1 Corinthians 10:13 makes four promises. What are they, and how does the promise of *"a way to escape"* change the way a believer thinks about the moment of temptation?

15. The chapter names three defenses against the three moves: rootedness in the Word, trust in God's character, and contentment in what God has given. How does each defense answer the move it is paired with?

REFERENCES

1. On the Hebrew *arum* and its use in Genesis 3:1, see Gordon J. Wenham, Genesis 1-15, Word Biblical Commentary (Waco: Word Books, 1987).

2. On the structure of the temptation narrative in Genesis 3 as a three-part sequence, see Walter Brueggemann, Genesis, Interpretation (Atlanta: John Knox Press, 1982).

3. On the correspondence between 1 John 2:16 and Genesis 3, see I. Howard Marshall, The Epistles of John, New International Commentary on the New Testament (Grand Rapids: Eerdmans, 1978).

4. On James 1:14-15 and the internal mechanism of temptation, see Peter Davids, The Epistle of James, New International Greek Testament Commentary (Grand Rapids: Eerdmans, 1982).

5. On the wilderness temptation of Jesus and His scriptural responses, see D. A. Carson, Matthew, Expositor's Bible Commentary (Grand Rapids: Zondervan, 1984).

6. On 1 Corinthians 10:13 and the way of escape, see Gordon D. Fee, The First Epistle to the Corinthians, New International Commentary on the New Testament (Grand Rapids: Eerdmans, 1987).

CHAPTER SEVEN

The Accuser of the Brethren

"And he shewed me Joshua the high priest standing before the angel of the LORD, and Satan standing at his right hand to resist him. And the LORD said unto Satan, The LORD rebuke thee, O Satan; even the LORD that hath chosen Jerusalem rebuke thee: is not this a brand plucked out of the fire? Now Joshua was clothed with filthy garments, and stood before the angel. And he answered and spake unto those that stood before him, saying, Take away the filthy garments from him. And unto him he said, Behold, I have caused thine iniquity to pass from thee, and I will clothe thee with change of raiment." (Zechariah 3:1-5)

In this passage, the prophet Zechariah is given a vision of a courtroom. The high priest Joshua stands before the angel of the LORD. Satan stands at Joshua's right hand. The Hebrew text uses *ha-Satan*, the title that means the Adversary. He is in his courtroom posture, in his courtroom function. Joshua is wearing filthy garments. The Adversary has a case to make against him.

The previous chapter took up the Adversary's strategy against the unbeliever and the seeking soul. Temptation is his work to bring a person down. This chapter takes up the second half of his work. Accusation is his work to keep a believer down. If he cannot stop the believer's coming to Christ, he will spend the rest of our lives trying to convince us that Christ does not really want us now that we are here.

A young Christian needs to be ready for this. The temptation phase, is loud and obvious. The accusation phase, after salvation, is quieter and more relentless. It can run for decades. It can make a believer who has been justified by the blood of Christ live as though we have not been. It can rob us of joy, of confidence in prayer, of usefulness in the church, of boldness in our daily walk with Christ. It is one of the Adversary's most successful operations against the people of God, and most believers do not even know what is happening to them while it is happening.

What Accusation Looks Like

Accusation is not the same as conviction. The distinction is vital because the believer has to learn to tell them apart.

Conviction is the work of the Holy Spirit through the word of God. John 16:8 says the Spirit, when He has come, *"will reprove the world of sin, and of righteousness, and of judgment."* The Greek verb here means to convict, to expose, to bring to light. Conviction names a specific sin. It points to a specific remedy. It produces godly sorrow. It leads to repentance and restoration. 2 Corinthians 7:10 makes the distinction directly: *"For godly sorrow worketh repentance to salvation not to be repented of: but the sorrow of the world worketh death."*

Accusation looks similar at first. It also focuses on sin. But it operates differently. Accusation is general rather than specific. It does not name a particular sin and offer a particular remedy. It tells you that you, as a person, are unworthy. It does not lead toward Christ. It leads away from Him. It does not produce repentance. It produces despair. It does not restore the relationship. It widens the distance.

The clearest practical test is the direction the voice points you. The word of the Spirit, even when it is sharp, points you toward the cross. The voice of the Adversary, even when it sounds spiritual, points you away from the cross. One says, "You sinned, here is what you did, here is the blood of Christ that cleanses it." The other says, "You sinned, you are unworthy, you should be ashamed, do not bother coming to Him with this." Same opening line. Different direction. Learn to feel the direction the voice is pointing you, and you will know which voice it is.

Accusation is also typically nocturnal. It rises in the quiet moments. It rises at night when the body is tired and the mind is unguarded. It rises after a failure, when the conscience is already raw. It rises before a moment of significant ministry or witness, when the believer is about to be useful. The timing is part of the strategy. The Adversary knows when to strike.

The Heavenly Court of Job 1 and 2

The most extended picture in Scripture of what accusation looks like is in Job 1-2. The Adversary's first move against Job is not to inflict suffering directly. It is to bring an accusation in the heavenly court about why Job serves God.

> *"Doth Job fear God for nought? Hast not thou made an hedge about him, and about his house, and about all that he hath on every side? thou hast blessed the work of his hands, and his substance is increased in the land. But put forth thine hand now, and touch all that he hath, and he will curse thee to thy face."* (Job 1:9-11)

The accusation in Job is interesting because it is not directly an accusation against Job. It is an accusation against the genuineness of Job's faith. The Adversary asks why Job serves God, and supplies his own answer: because God has paid him to. Take away the rewards, and the relationship will be exposed as a transaction.

This is one of the Adversary's deeper accusations. He does not always accuse believers of specific sins. Sometimes he accuses them of motives. Of being interested in God only for what God provides. Of being religious for social reasons or family reasons or guilt reasons rather than from genuine love for God. **The accusation is designed to shake the believer's confidence not in behavior but in our actual relationship with God.**

The Lord's response in Job is illuminating. He does not deny that Job has a hedge around him, that God has blessed him, that his substance is increased in the land. All of that is true. What He denies is the Adversary's interpretation. He gives the

Adversary permission to test the interpretation, with limits. And the test, painful as it was for Job, ends with the Adversary's interpretation thoroughly destroyed. Job did not serve God for the rewards. He served God because God was God.

Look at what this story tells us as followers of God. The Adversary will sometimes accuse you, in the quiet of your own thoughts, of not really loving God. Of "going to church" for the wrong reasons. Of praying for selfish reasons. Of obeying because you are afraid of consequences rather than because you love the One who gave the commands. The accusation may have a grain of truth in it, because mixed motives are part of being human. But the Adversary will use the grain of truth to suggest that the whole relationship is fake. That is the lie. A believer with mixed motives is still a believer. The Lord works through mixed motives to refine pure ones over time. The Adversary wants you to throw out the whole relationship because it is not yet perfect. The Lord wants you to keep coming, and to let Him perfect what is incomplete.

The Pattern in Zechariah 3

Return now to the scene that opened this chapter. Zechariah 3 is shorter than Job, but it is even more compressed and even more revealing about the gospel's answer to accusation.

Joshua the high priest is standing before the angel of the LORD. He is wearing filthy garments. The Adversary is at his right hand, in the position of the prosecutor. The case looks easy. Joshua is the high priest of the people, and his garments are filthy. He is unfit to stand in this position. The accusation does not even need to be spoken. The evidence is on his clothing.

But notice what the Lord does. He does not defend Joshua's record. He does not deny that the garments are filthy. He does not minimize the case the Adversary is bringing. Instead, He silences the Adversary with a rebuke (*"The LORD rebuke thee, O Satan"*), and then He acts. He commands that the filthy garments be removed and that Joshua be clothed with change of raiment. He says, *"Behold, I have caused thine iniquity to pass from thee."*

The pattern here is the gospel in miniature. The accusation is not denied. The evidence is not disputed. The believer's filthy garments are real. But the Lord answers the accusation by providing what the accusation said was missing. He removes the filth. He clothes the believer in clean garments. The case the Adversary brought is answered not by argument but by a gift.

This pattern will appear again in Romans 8 and in Revelation 12. Joshua's vision is the Old Testament template. The Accuser brings a true charge. The Lord covers the believer with what the Accuser said was lacking. The believer stands clean, not because the charge was false, but because the Lord has provided the answer to the charge.

Take this pattern personally. When the Adversary brings an accusation against you, the answer is not, "I am not really that bad." The answer is, "Yes, that is true about me, and the blood of Christ has covered it. The Lord has caused mine iniquity to pass from me. I am clothed with His love and mercy." That is the right answer. It is also the only answer that actually works against accusation. Every other answer either denies the truth of the charge (which the Adversary will keep pressing because the charge is true) or accepts the charge without the gospel (which produces the despair the Adversary is aiming for). The gospel answer admits the charge and points to the Lamb.

Sifting in Luke 22

Jesus says something remarkable to Peter on the night of the Last Supper.

> *"And the Lord said, Simon, Simon, behold, Satan hath desired to have you, that he may sift you as wheat: But I have prayed for thee, that thy faith fail not: and when thou art converted, strengthen thy brethren."* (Luke 22:31-32)

Several details require attention. Satan asked permission to sift Peter. The verb "desired" can be translated as "demanded" or "obtained by asking." The Adversary's access to a believer requires divine permission, as it did with Job. Jesus prayed specifically for Peter, not that the test would not happen, but that Peter's faith would not finally fail. And Jesus assumed Peter would come back, and assumed that his coming back would equip him to strengthen the brethren.

The pattern is important. Satan has access to test believers, but only with permission. Jesus prays for the specific believer being tested. The faith may waver but does not finally fail. The believer who comes through the test has something to give other believers facing similar tests.

Peter denied Christ three times that night. He went out and wept bitterly. He thought he had failed beyond recovery. He had not. The Lord found him on the shore of the Sea of Galilee, asked him three times if he loved Him, restored him three times, and commissioned him to feed His sheep. The very experience that the Adversary had used to try to destroy Peter became the experience that made him useful to the early church for the rest of his life.

A young believer needs this picture in our heads. There will be moments when the Adversary's accusations will seem proven. You will fall in some way. You will think you have lost your standing with God. You will hear, in your own mind, the voice that says, "There is no coming back from this. You have shown what you really are. Christ has no use for you anymore." That voice is a lie. Peter heard the same voice the morning of the resurrection. He was wrong, and so are you. The Lord has prayed for you. Your faith may waver. It will not finally fail, because His prayer has not failed. And the experience of falling and being restored will be one of the most useful experiences of your life. You will be able to strengthen the brethren in a way you never could have before.

Romans 8 and the Closed Court

Paul gives the most decisive answer to accusation in Romans 8:33-34:

> *"Who shall lay any thing to the charge of God's elect? It is God that justifieth. Who is he that condemneth? It is Christ that died, yea*

> *rather, that is risen again, who is even at the right hand of God, who also maketh intercession for us."*

Notice the structure of Paul's argument. The questions are rhetorical. "Who shall lay any thing to the charge of God's elect?" The expected answer is no one, because God Himself has already declared the believer righteous. "Who is he that condemneth?" The expected answer is no one, because Christ has died, risen, and now intercedes at the right hand of God.

The Accuser's voice is silenced not by denying the charges but by pointing to the One who has answered them. Justification is not a matter of being innocent. It is a matter of being declared righteous on the basis of what Christ has done. The believer's standing before God does not depend on the absence of accusations against us. It depends on the work of the One who has answered every accusation in advance.

This is why a Christian can stand confidently against accusation without becoming spiritually careless. The basis of confidence is not, "I am not that bad." The basis is, "I have been justified by the blood of Christ." The first basis is fragile and false. The second is unshakable and true.

There is also a courtroom geography that matters here. The Adversary's name in Greek, *diabolos*, slanderer, comes from the practice of throwing accusations across a court. He throws charges against believers before God. But in Romans 8 the court has been reordered. The Judge has already declared the verdict. The convicted criminal is at the right hand of the Judge as the believer's intercessor. The Accuser's case has been mooted before he opens his mouth. He still throws charges. But the charges fall in a court that has already closed.

This image is one to put firmly in your head. When you are facing accusation in your mind, picture the court. The Judge is on the throne. The verdict has been entered. You have been declared righteous in Christ. The One who paid for that righteousness is standing beside you as your advocate. The Accuser is in the corner of the room throwing paper that no one is reading. That is the actual situation.

The accusation feels weighty because the Accuser is loud, but the case has already been decided.

Revelation 12 and the Overcomers

Revelation 12:10-11 closes the picture: "

> *Now is come salvation, and strength, and the kingdom of our God, and the power of his Christ: for the accuser of our brethren is cast down, which accused them before our God day and night. And they overcame him by the blood of the Lamb, and by the word of their testimony; and they loved not their lives unto the death."*

Three observations here.

First, the title *"the accuser of our brethren"* is one of Satan's primary designations. Accusation is not a side activity for him. It is what he does. "Day and night" describes the constancy of the operation. He does not rest. He does not take periodic breaks. The accusation continues whether or not anyone is listening.

Second, the believers in this passage overcome him. Their victory is described in three components. The blood of the Lamb. The word of their testimony. The willingness to lose their lives for the truth.

The blood of the Lamb is the objective foundation. It is the work of Christ that has actually answered the charges in the heavenly court. Without this foundation, no overcoming is possible.

The word of their testimony is the subjective application. It is the believer's verbal acknowledgment of what the blood has accomplished. The verbal naming matters. The believer who says aloud what Christ has done for us is engaging the Accuser on different terms. The Accuser brings charges. The believer points to the Lamb. The Accuser brings more charges. The believer points again. The verbal testimony, repeated, brings the objective work into the subjective experience.

The third component is the willingness to lose one's life rather than capitulate to the Accuser. This is the deepest level of resistance. The Accuser's deepest leverage is the threat that yielding to him is necessary for self-preservation. The believer who has settled in advance that we would rather die than capitulate has removed the Accuser's leverage entirely. Note that this does not mean we will die. It means we have decided in advance that we would rather die than turn from Christ, and that decision changes everything about how the Accuser's threats land.

A young believer can begin practicing this third component long before we ever face the kind of test it was originally written about. Every time you decide you would rather take the social cost than deny Christ, you are practicing this. Every time you keep your stand on something Scripture has settled, even when the people around you are pressing you to soften it, you are practicing this. The willingness to lose your life is built up in small decisions long before it is ever tested in the largest one.

The three components together are the believer's complete answer to the Accuser. The blood of the Lamb is the foundation. The word of testimony is the application. The willingness to lose one's life is the proof that the believer is not in the relationship with Christ for what we can get out of it. The Adversary's accusation in Job 1 has been definitively refuted, in this passage, by countless believers across history. The Accuser's case has been answered.

Practical Steps for the Accused Believer

A young believer being attacked by accusation can take specific steps to resist.

First, name what is happening. The voice that accuses you is not God. It is not your conscience. It is the Adversary doing what the Bible says he does. Naming it strips it of some of its power. The voice that pretends to be your own thoughts is not your own thoughts. It is an Adversary operating in a way Scripture has explicitly described.

Second, answer the accusation with the gospel rather than with self-defense. Do not try to argue that you are not as bad as the accusation says. Some of the time, the accusation is accurate about the facts. The defense is not, "I am not that bad." The defense is, "Yes, and the blood of Christ has covered it."

Third, get the testimony out of your head and into the air. Speak the truth aloud. Read the relevant Scripture aloud. The verbal naming matters because it engages the Accuser in the verbal arena where the contest is actually happening.

Fourth, refuse to entertain the accusation in private. Bring it into the light. Tell a trusted Christian friend or a mature believer in your church about what you are facing. The Adversary works in isolation. Light reduces his effectiveness.

Fifth, return to the cross. Read about it. Sing about it. Take the Lord's Supper. The cross is the central evidence of God's answer to the accusations against you. The more time you spend with the evidence, the less you will be moved by accusations the evidence has already answered.

These are not magic formulas. They are practices. Practices, repeated over years, build the kind of believer who can stand against the Accuser without being moved. Build the practices now. You will need them later.

What This Chapter Establishes

One. Accusation is one of the Adversary's primary activities against believers, distinct from temptation. Temptation aims to bring a person down. Accusation aims to keep a believer down.

Two. Accusation must be distinguished from the conviction of the Holy Spirit. Conviction names specific sins, points to specific remedies, and leads to repentance. Accusation is general, points away from Christ, and produces despair.

Three. Job 1-2 shows the Adversary accusing the genuineness of a believer's faith. Zechariah 3 shows the Adversary accusing a believer of unworthiness, and shows the Lord's answer through the changing of garments.

Four. Luke 22 shows the Adversary's access requires permission, Christ's intercession is specific, and the believer who comes through the test is equipped to strengthen others.

Five. Romans 8:33-34 closes the heavenly court against accusation by pointing to the work of Christ. The Accuser still throws charges, but the charges fall in a court that has already issued its verdict.

Six. Revelation 12:10-11 names the believer's three-part victory over the Accuser: the blood of the Lamb, the word of testimony, and the willingness to lose one's life.

Review Questions

1. Zechariah 3:1-5 shows Satan standing at the right hand of Joshua the high priest *"to resist him."* What is the courtroom posture being described, and what does the Hebrew title *ha-Satan* mean?

2. The chapter distinguishes between the conviction of the Holy Spirit and the accusation of the Adversary. What are the differences in how each one operates, and how can a believer tell them apart?

3. The chapter says accusation is typically nocturnal. Why does the Adversary tend to bring accusations in quiet moments, after failures, or before significant ministry?

4. In Job 1-2, the Adversary's accusation is not against Job's behavior but against his motives. How does this kind of accusation work against believers today?

5. The Lord's response to Job's situation does not deny the facts the Adversary cited but exposes the false interpretation. How does this model how believers should respond to accusations against their motives?

6. In Zechariah 3, the Lord answers the accusation against Joshua by removing his filthy garments and clothing him in clean ones. How is this the gospel in miniature?

7. The chapter says the right answer to accusation is not "I am not really that bad" but "Yes, and the blood of Christ has covered it." Why is this distinction important?

8. In Luke 22:31-32, Jesus tells Peter that Satan has desired to sift him but that Jesus has prayed for him. What does this passage establish about the Adversary's access to believers and the Lord's response to that access?

9. Peter denied Christ three times yet was restored and equipped to strengthen the brethren. What does Peter's experience tell a young believer about the relationship between failure and future usefulness?

10. Romans 8:33-34 silences the Accuser by pointing to the work of Christ. How does Paul's argument show that justification provides a basis for confidence that personal innocence cannot provide?

11. The chapter describes a courtroom geography in which the verdict has already been entered, the Accuser is throwing charges in a closed court. How does this image change the way a believer should respond to accusatory thoughts?

12. Revelation 12:10-11 says believers overcome the Accuser *"by the blood of the Lamb, and by the word of their testimony; and they loved not their lives unto the death."* How do these three components work together, and what role does each play in defeating accusation?

13. The chapter says the willingness to lose one's life is built up in small decisions long before it is tested in the largest one. What does this look like in the daily life of a young Christian?

14. The chapter ends with five practical steps for the accused believer. Walk through each one and explain how it engages the Accuser on the right ground.

REFERENCES

1. On Zechariah 3 as a courtroom scene and the gospel's answer to accusation, see Joyce G. Baldwin, Haggai, Zechariah, Malachi, Tyndale Old Testament Commentaries (Downers Grove: IVP Academic, 1972).

2. On the Adversary's accusation in Job 1-2 and the testing of faith, see John E. Hartley, The Book of Job, New International Commentary on the Old Testament (Grand Rapids: Eerdmans, 1988).

3. On Luke 22:31-32 and the sifting of Peter, see I. Howard Marshall, The Gospel of Luke, New International Greek Testament Commentary (Grand Rapids: Eerdmans, 1978).

4. On Romans 8:33-34 and the closed court of accusation, see Douglas J. Moo, The Epistle to the Romans, New International Commentary on the New Testament (Grand Rapids: Eerdmans, 1996).

5. On Revelation 12:10-11 and the threefold overcoming, see G. K. Beale, The Book of Revelation, New International Greek Testament Commentary (Grand Rapids: Eerdmans, 1999).

6. On the distinction between conviction and accusation in spiritual experience, see John Owen, The Works of John Owen, Volume 6: Temptation and Sin (London: Banner of Truth Trust, 1965).

CHAPTER EIGHT

Principalities and Powers

"Then said he unto me, Fear not, Daniel: for from the first day that thou didst set thine heart to understand, and to chasten thyself before thy God, thy words were heard, and I am come for thy words. But the prince of the kingdom of Persia withstood me one and twenty days: but, lo, Michael, one of the chief princes, came to help me; and I remained there with the kings of Persia." (Daniel 10:12-13)

The prophet Daniel has been fasting and praying for three weeks. An angelic messenger finally arrives with the answer to his prayer. The angel explains the delay. He had been opposed by *"the prince of the kingdom of Persia"* for twenty-one days, until Michael, one of the chief princes, came to help. The angel speaks of these spiritual figures matter-of-factly, as known features of the unseen realm.

This passage is one of the clearest windows in the Old Testament into the structured organization of the Adversary's forces. There are princes assigned to specific kingdoms. There are conflicts between angelic beings of different allegiances. There are figures of higher rank, like Michael, who can intervene to break stalemates. The unseen realm is not chaotic. It has a structure. The fallen side has an organization. The faithful side has an organization. They contend.

The previous chapter took up the Adversary's accusation of believers. This chapter takes up the structure of his organization. He does not work alone. The fallen angels who fell with him in the original rebellion are arranged in some kind of hierarchy, with specific assignments and specific functions. Scripture does not give us a complete organizational chart, but it gives us enough to understand that the opposition is structured, intelligent, and coordinated.

We need this picture, but we also need to be careful with it. The history of Christian writing on this subject contains some of the most accurate biblical exposition and some of the most fanciful speculation in the Christian tradition. Medieval grimoires, modern deliverance manuals, and books that claim detailed knowledge of demonic hierarchies have produced material that goes well past anything in Scripture. This chapter holds the line at what the text actually establishes.

Ephesians 6:12 and the Four Categories

The clearest single statement on the structure of the fallen realm is Ephesians 6:12:

> *"For we wrestle not against flesh and blood, but against principalities, against powers, against the rulers of the darkness of this world, against spiritual wickedness in high places."*

Paul names four categories of opposition. The Greek words are *archai* (principalities), *exousiai* (powers or authorities), *kosmokratores* (world-rulers, literally cosmic-rulers of this darkness), and *pneumatika tes ponerias en tois epouraniois* (spiritual forces of evil in the heavenly places).

Each term carries specific meaning.

Archai refers to rulers, beginnings, or first ones. The word is used in Greek literature for leaders or those holding authority. Within the fallen hierarchy, these appear to be high-ranking figures with broad jurisdiction. The same word is used positively in Colossians 1:16 of created beings who serve God, which suggests that these categories existed in the original heavenly order before the fall, and that some beings in each category fell with Satan.

Exousiai refers to authorities or powers. The word denotes the right to exercise power, suggesting these are figures whose function is the exercise of delegated authority within the fallen system. Like *archai*, this term is used in both heavenly and fallen contexts.

Kosmokratores is more striking. The literal sense is "world-rulers" or "rulers of the cosmos." Paul qualifies it with "of this darkness," limiting the rule to the fallen order in its current state. These figures appear to govern the broad systems of the world that operate in opposition to God.

Pneumatika tes ponerias en tois epouraniois names spiritual forces of wickedness in the heavenly places. The phrase *"heavenly places"* (*epouranios*) is used elsewhere in Ephesians for the realm where Christ is seated (Ephesians 1:20) and where believers are blessed in Him (Ephesians 1:3). The fallen forces operate in an overlapping sphere. The conflict is not on a different plane from where Christ rules. It is in the same realm, with the outcome already settled but the fighting still in progress.

Look at what these four terms add up to. They describe a graded organization, from broad cosmic rulers down to localized authorities. The Adversary is not running a flat operation. He has a chain of command. He has assignments. He has districts. He has specialists. The believer is not facing a generic spiritual threat. We are facing an organized opposition.

This does not mean the believer needs to identify which category is opposing us in any given situation. Paul does not give the categories so that we can name them in our prayer requests. He gives the categories so that we understand the scale and seriousness of what we are facing. The point is not, "I am wrestling with an exousia today." The point is, "What I am wrestling with is not flesh and blood. It is part of an organized opposition. I need spiritual armor, not natural human responses."

Daniel 10 and Territorial Spirits

Daniel 10 gives the clearest example of how this hierarchy operates in geographic terms. The angelic messenger refers to *"the prince of the kingdom of Persia"* who withstood him for twenty-one days. He later mentions *"the prince of Grecia"* (Daniel 10:20). Michael is described as *"one of the chief princes"* and as *"your prince"* with reference to the people of Israel (Daniel 10:21).

These references suggest that specific spiritual beings are associated with specific nations or kingdoms. Persia has a prince. Greece has a prince. Israel has Michael. The implication is that the spiritual conflict has a geographic structure that mirrors, in some way, the political map.

This concept has been called territorial spirits in some modern Christian writing, and the concept itself has biblical support. What does not have biblical support is the elaborate practice some have built around it, where believers are taught to identify the specific spirits over their cities, name them, and bind them in prayer. Scripture neither commands nor models this practice. The Bible's response to the territorial structure of evil is straightforward. Pray for the people. Preach the gospel. Trust the Lord to handle the spiritual warfare at its proper level. Daniel did not bind the prince of Persia. He fasted, prayed, sought the Lord, and the conflict above his level was handled by Michael and the angelic messenger.

A young person should take special note of this lesson. There are real spiritual realities operating in the cultures and nations we live in. They are above our pay grade. The Lord has not given us a commission to engage them directly. He has given us a commission to walk faithfully with Him, to pray for the people around us, to spread the gospel, and to trust Him to handle what we cannot see. The believers who try to take on more than the Lord has assigned them often end up either exhausted or deceived. The believer who walks faithfully in our assigned role becomes, by that faithfulness, a quiet but real opposition to the territorial powers around us. That is the pattern Scripture actually models.

Jude 6 and the Imprisoned Angels

Not all of the original fallen angels are currently active. Jude 1:6 says: *"And the angels which kept not their first estate, but left their own habitation, he hath reserved in everlasting chains under darkness unto the judgment of the great day."*

2 Peter 2:4 makes the same point: *"For if God spared not the angels that sinned, but cast them down to hell, and delivered them into chains of darkness, to be reserved unto judgment."*

Some category of fallen angels has already been removed from operation. They are restrained, awaiting final judgment. The exact nature of their offense and the timing of their imprisonment are subjects of long-standing interpretive debate. Some readers connect these passages to the obscure account in Genesis 6 of "*the sons of God*" who took human wives. Scripture does not support this silly notion of fallen angels marrying human women. Others read the passages as referring to the original angelic rebellion in general. Scripture simply does not settle the question.

What the passages do settle is the principle. The Adversary's forces are smaller than the original rebellion produced. Some have been removed from the field. The Lord has the authority to imprison fallen angels, has done so in some cases, and will judge all of them at the appointed time. The fallen hierarchy is not unlimited in its membership or in its time of operation.

This is encouraging. The opposition the Chirstian faces is real but bounded. The fallen angels still operating are operating under permission and under limits. They have not multiplied since the original rebellion. They cannot reproduce. Their numbers are fixed and, in some cases, reduced. The Adversary's army is not growing. The army of the Lord, by contrast, is growing every day, every time another sinner is brought out of darkness and into the kingdom.

1 Timothy 4:1 and Doctrines of Demons

> *"Now the Spirit speaketh expressly, that in the latter times some shall depart from the faith, giving heed to seducing spirits, and doctrines of devils."* (1 Timothy 4:1)

The phrase "doctrines of devils" is striking. The Greek *didaskaliai daimonion* means teachings that are associated with or pertain to demons. Paul is saying that some who depart from the faith do so by attending to teachings that have a demonic source.

The implication for the believer is twofold. First, doctrinal carefulness is a form of spiritual warfare. The believer who tests teachings against Scripture (1 John 4:1) is not engaged in a merely intellectual exercise. We are engaged in resisting the work of the fallen hierarchy. Second, the believer who teaches others has a heightened responsibility, because the same hierarchy is working to introduce false teachings through whatever channels are open. James 3:1 warns that those who teach incur a stricter judgment, and one of the reasons is the spiritual stakes.

We should think hard about what we allow into our minds as teaching. Books. Podcasts. Sermons. Social media accounts. So-called Christian music or worship songs. All of these are channels for doctrine, and not all doctrine is from God. The test is Scripture. Whatever does not align with what Scripture says is suspect, regardless of how appealing the teacher is, how popular the source is, or how widely accepted the teaching has become. The Christian who develops the habit of testing what we hear against the actual text of Scripture, is the believer who will not be carried off by the doctrines of demons.

A Word About Modern Speculation

The territory of demonic hierarchy has produced more speculative writing than almost any other area of Christian theology. Medieval grimoires like the Ars Goetia and the Lesser Key of Solomon claim to list specific demons by name and to provide instructions for invoking and binding them. Some modern "Christian" writers have produced equally detailed material about the names, ranks, and territorial assignments of demonic beings. Both of these groups go far past anything Scripture supports.

The practical danger of this material is twofold. The first danger is engagement. The believer who reads detailed material about demonic names and rankings is engaging with a level of detail Scripture has not supplied, often through sources that are not spiritually safe. The medieval grimoires, in particular, are not Christian works. They are occult works masquerading as Christian. To consult them is to expose oneself to influence from the very forces they claim to control.

The second danger is fascination. The believer who develops a strong interest in the details of demonic hierarchy has, in some sense, allowed our attention to be diverted. The Adversary is happy to be the object of detailed study, especially if the study replaces what should have been time spent in the Word and in prayer. The Christian who knows the names of two hundred demons and can recite their ranks but cannot tell someone what to do to be saved, has misallocated their attention.

The biblical pattern is to know enough about the Adversary to recognize his work and to resist him, and then to turn the bulk of attention to Christ, to the Word, to the church, and to the work the Lord has assigned. The Adversary is not the center of Scripture's attention. He should not be the center of ours.

The Hierarchy and the Ordinary Believer

The young believer reading this chapter may wonder what difference the existence of a demonic hierarchy makes to us ordinary life. The answer is in three parts.

First, the hierarchy explains the persistence and intelligence of opposition. When you find that the same temptations come back at predictable times, that resistance to your spiritual growth has the feel of organized strategy rather than random pressure, that certain ideas seem to find you again and again no matter how many times you have rejected them, you are encountering the work of an organized opposition. You are not paranoid. You are not making it up. Ephesians 6:12 has named the situation. The opposition is real, and it is structured.

Second, the hierarchy underscores the necessity of armor. Paul does not name the four categories of opposition in order to alarm believers. He names them in the same passage where he commands the putting on of the armor of God (Ephesians 6:13-17). The armor is not a metaphor for self-improvement. It is the actual provision the Lord has made for the actual conflict. Chapter Twelve will go through the armor in detail.

Third, the hierarchy points to the centrality of Christ. Colossians 2:15 says that Christ "*spoiled principalities and powers*" at the cross, "*triumphing over them in it.*" The same hierarchies named in Ephesians 6 were defeated in Colossians 2. The believer's standing in this conflict does not depend on us ability to identify specific spiritual forces. It depends on the work of the One who has already defeated the entire hierarchy. Chapter Eleven will go through this in detail.

The Christian's job is not to engage the hierarchy at our own level. Our job is to stand in Christ, who has already defeated the hierarchy on us behalf. We walk in His victory. We do not generate our own. The opposition that comes to us has already been answered before we ever encounter it. Our resistance is not a fresh fight against fresh enemies. It is the application, in our specific circumstances, of a victory that was won at Calvary and ratified at the empty tomb.

How the Hierarchy Operates Against the Church

Look at how the hierarchy operates against the church specifically. The opposition is not random. It is targeted at what matters most to the work of God in the world.

The first target is the Word of God. Every age of the church has seen attacks on the trustworthiness of Scripture, the authority of Scripture, and the meaning of Scripture. These attacks come in waves, often led by figures who present themselves as "Christian thinkers" offering helpful corrections. The pattern is the same as the Serpent's question in Genesis 3. Hath God really said? In every era, the form of the question changes. The substance does not. The hierarchy keeps pressing because the Word is the believer's primary defense, and if the Word can be loosened in the believer's mind, everything else becomes easier to attack.

The second target is unity. Jesus prayed in John 17 that His followers would be one as He and the Father are one. The unity of the church is part of the power of the gospel. The hierarchy works tirelessly to fracture that unity. Sometimes through doctrinal disputes that should have been resolvable. Sometimes through personality conflicts that get inflated past their actual size. Sometimes through cultural pressures that drive wedges between believers who should have been able to stand together. Satan does not care which fracture line opens up. He just wants the fracture.

The third target is the mission. Wherever the gospel is going forward, the hierarchy mobilizes resistance. Missionaries report it. Church planters report it. Believers who are reaching their unbelieving friends report it. The resistance takes different forms in different settings, but the pattern is consistent. The harder you push toward unreached people with the gospel, the more organized the opposition becomes. This is not paranoia. It is what Paul described when he said in 1 Thessalonians 2:18, *"we would have come unto you, even I Paul, once and again; but Satan hindered us."* The Adversary actively strives to hinder the spread of the gospel.

The fourth target is the next generation. Satan works to keep young people from receiving the faith of their parents. Sometimes through outright hostility to Christianity in the surrounding culture. Sometimes through the more subtle work of making faith look embarrassing or naive. Sometimes through the formation of a peer culture that punishes any visible commitment to Christ. The reason for the focus on young people is obvious. The Adversary knows that a generation lost to Christ now is a generation that will not raise the next generation in Christ. He thinks long-term. The believer who walks faithfully through our young years has done something with significant downstream consequences, even if we cannot see them yet.

Knowing these four targets equips the Christian to recognize when we are in the line of fire. If you are loving the Word of God, working for unity in your church, sharing the gospel with someone, or living visibly as a faithful Christian, you can and should expect resistance. The resistance is evidence you are doing something the hierarchy is interested in stopping. The Lord has not promised the absence of resistance. He has promised the presence of His grace and help through it.

The Difference Between Awareness and Obsession

Paul's letters are interesting for what they include and what they leave out. He names the principalities and powers. He commands the wearing of the armor. He warns against the wiles of the Devil. But he does not give the Ephesian believers detailed instructions for naming, binding, or warring against specific demons. He gives them Christ, the Word, prayer, and the church. That is the equipment list. The equipment is absolutely sufficient. The equipment was sufficient for the apostolic generation, and it is 100% sufficient for ours.

A young Christian should aim for awareness of the hierarchy of Satan without having an obsession with it. Awareness means understanding that the conflict is real and structured. Obsession means making the hierarchy a primary subject of study, prayer, and conversation. The first is biblical and useful. The second is unbalanced and tends to produce believers who are spiritually anxious rather than spiritually steady.

The mark of a believer who has the right balance is that we take the Adversary seriously without being preoccupied by him. We know he is real. We know his methods. We know the armor. We walk confidently in Christ, ready for the conflict but not consumed by it.

What This Chapter Establishes

One. The Adversary's forces are organized, with a hierarchy and assignments described in Scripture in specific terms.

Two. Ephesians 6:12 names four categories of opposition: *archai*, *exousiai*, *kosmokratores*, and *pneumatika tes ponerias*. Each describes a level or function within the fallen hierarchy.

Three. Daniel 10 shows that the spiritual conflict has a geographic structure, with specific princes associated with specific kingdoms. The biblical response is faithfulness in one's assigned role, not direct engagement with territorial spirits at one's own initiative.

Four. Jude 1:6 and 2 Peter 2:4 establish that some fallen angels have already been imprisoned. The Adversary's forces are bounded and, in some cases, reduced.

Five. 1 Timothy 4:1 connects the fallen hierarchy to false teaching. The doctrines of devils are part of the Adversary's work, and doctrinal carefulness is a form of spiritual resistance.

Six. The believer's response to the hierarchy is awareness without obsession. We know the structure exists, takes the conflict seriously, puts on the armor, and walks in the victory Christ has already won. We do not engage at our own level or develop a fascination with details Scripture has not supplied.

Review Questions

1. Daniel 10:12-13 describes a delay of twenty-one days as the angelic messenger contended with *"the prince of the kingdom of Persia."* What does this passage establish about the structure and reality of spiritual conflict?

2. Ephesians 6:12 names four categories: *archai* (principalities), *exousiai* (powers), *kosmokratores* (world-rulers), and *pneumatika tes ponerias en tois epouraniois* (spiritual wickedness in the heavenly places). What does each term describe?

3. The chapter says Paul gives the four categories not so we can identify which one is opposing us in prayer requests but so we understand the scale of the opposition. What is the practical difference?

4. Daniel 10 mentions the prince of Persia, the prince of Greece, and Michael as the prince associated with Israel. What does this geographic structure tell us about how spiritual conflict relates to political and national realities?

5. The chapter argues that Daniel did not bind the prince of Persia but fasted and prayed. What does this model for believers today regarding direct engagement with territorial spirits?

6. Jude 1:6 and 2 Peter 2:4 describe certain fallen angels as already imprisoned. How does this fact bound the opposition believers face today?

7. The chapter argues that the Adversary's army is not growing while the army of the Lord grows daily. How does this perspective change the way a believer thinks about the long-term trajectory of spiritual conflict?

8. 1 Timothy 4:1 connects *"doctrines of devils"* (*didaskaliai daimonion*) to falling away from the faith. How does this passage make doctrinal carefulness a form of spiritual warfare?

9. The chapter warns against medieval grimoires like the Ars Goetia and modern detailed treatments of demonic hierarchies. What is the practical danger of this material, and how should a believer relate to it?

10. The chapter says some Christians have a fascination with demonic detail that has misallocated their attention. What is the right balance between knowing enough about the Adversary and being preoccupied with him?

11. Colossians 2:15 says Christ *"spoiled principalities and powers"* at the cross. How does this verse change the believer's posture in the spiritual conflict?

12. The chapter says the believer's job is not to engage the hierarchy at our own level but to stand in Christ's already-won victory. What does this look like in daily Christian life?

13. The chapter contrasts awareness of the hierarchy with obsession about it. What does the right posture look like, and how does it produce a steady rather than anxious believer?

14. Paul's letters name the principalities and powers and command the armor of God but do not give detailed instructions for naming or binding specific demons. What does the apostolic equipment list tell us about what is necessary and sufficient for the believer's walk in spiritual conflict?

REFERENCES

1. On Daniel 10 and the territorial structure of spiritual conflict, see John E. Goldingay, Daniel, Word Biblical Commentary (Dallas: Word Books, 1989).

2. On Ephesians 6:12 and the four categories of opposition, see Andrew T. Lincoln, Ephesians, Word Biblical Commentary (Dallas: Word Books, 1990).

3. On the meaning of *archai*, *exousiai*, *kosmokratores*, and pneumatika in Pauline usage, see Clinton E. Arnold, Powers of Darkness: Principalities and Powers in Paul's Letters (Downers Grove: IVP Academic, 1992).

4. On Jude 1:6 and the imprisoned angels, see Thomas R. Schreiner, 1, 2 Peter, Jude, New American Commentary (Nashville: Broadman and Holman, 2003).

5. On 1 Timothy 4:1 and the doctrine of demons, see George W. Knight III, The Pastoral Epistles, New International Greek Testament Commentary (Grand Rapids: Eerdmans, 1992).

6. On Colossians 2:15 and Christ's triumph over the powers, see N. T. Wright, Colossians and Philemon, Tyndale New Testament Commentaries (Downers Grove: IVP Academic, 1986).

7. On the dangers of speculative writing about demonic hierarchies, see Sydney H. T. Page, Powers of Evil: A Biblical Study of Satan and Demons (Grand Rapids: Baker, 1995).

CHAPTER NINE

Demons in Scripture

"And they came over unto the other side of the sea, into the country of the Gadarenes. And when he was come out of the ship, immediately there met him out of the tombs a man with an unclean spirit, who had his dwelling among the tombs; and no man could bind him, no, not with chains: Because that he had been often bound with fetters and chains, and the chains had been plucked asunder by him, and the fetters broken in pieces: neither could any man tame him. And always, night and day, he was in the mountains, and in the tombs, crying, and cutting himself with stones. But when he saw Jesus afar off, he ran and worshipped him, And cried with a loud voice, and said, What have I to do with thee, Jesus, thou Son of the most high God? I adjure thee by God, that thou torment me not." (Mark 5:1-7)

The man at the tombs of the Gadarenes is one of the most extreme cases of demon possession Scripture records. He has been overtaken by an unclean spirit. He lives among the dead. He has supernatural strength that breaks chains. He cuts himself. He cries out night and day. He cannot be tamed. When Jesus arrives, the spirit recognizes Him at distance, names Him correctly, and pleads for mercy.

The previous chapter took up the structure of the Adversary's organization. This chapter takes the next step. What does Scripture say about demons in particular, what they did during the miraculous period when Christ and His apostles walked the earth, and what does this material mean for us living today? The territory of this subject has been worked over by Hollywood, by horror literature, by sensational ministry, and by occult writing. The cultural picture is, again, mostly wrong. The biblical picture is leaner, more specific, and more useful, but it has to be read with attention to what was happening then and what is happening now.

A young Christian needs to think clearly about this. The cultural picture of demon possession comes mainly from horror movies and from modern ministries that claim ongoing dramatic encounters with possessing spirits. The result is that most young Christians either think demons are entirely fictional (because the movies are obviously fiction) or they imagine that the dramatic encounters of the Gospels are still happening today and that they should expect to see them or even take part in them. Both pictures need correcting from the text of the Bible.

The Reality of Demonic Activity in the Biblical Period

Demons are real. The Gospels contain dozens of accounts of Jesus and the apostles encountering, casting out, and authoritatively addressing demonic beings. The book of Acts continues the pattern through the apostolic period. The epistles assume the reality of these beings and warn believers about their continued activity in specific ways.

A modern materialist worldview has trained many people, including many Christians, to be embarrassed about this material. The temptation is to reinterpret biblical accounts of demon possession as ancient descriptions of mental illness, epilepsy, or other physical conditions that the ancients did not have categories for.

This reinterpretation has a problem. Scripture itself distinguishes between demonic affliction and other illnesses. Matthew 4:24 lists separately *"those which were possessed with devils, and those which were lunatick, and those that had the palsy."* Mark 1:32-34 says Jesus healed many that were sick of various diseases and *"cast out many devils."* The biblical text treats demon possession as a real category distinct from medical conditions. Both were treated with seriousness, and Scripture distinguishes them carefully.

The question this chapter has to answer is what the relationship is between the dramatic biblical accounts and the experience of believers today. Does demon possession still happen in the way Scripture describes it? The honest biblical answer requires looking at what the New Testament says about the period it was describing, and what it says about the period that would follow.

The Miraculous Period and Its Purpose

The dramatic encounters with demons in the Gospels and Acts belong to a specific period in redemptive history. That period was the time of Christ's earthly ministry and the apostolic age that followed. During this period, miraculous gifts were active. Healings occurred. Unknown tongues were spoken. The dead were raised. And demons were cast out. These all absolutely happened.

The purpose of these miraculous works was specific. Hebrews 2:3-4 names it directly:

> *"How shall we escape, if we neglect so great salvation; which at the first began to be spoken by the Lord, and was confirmed unto us by them that heard him; God also bearing them witness, both with signs and wonders, and with divers miracles, and gifts of the Holy Ghost, according to his own will?"*

The miraculous works were the confirmation of the message. They bore witness to the truth of the gospel as it was being proclaimed for the first time.

Mark 16:20 says the same thing about the apostolic preaching: "

> *And they went forth, and preached every where, the Lord working with them, and confirming the word with signs following."*

The signs followed and confirmed the word. They were not given as ongoing equipment for every generation of believers. They were given to confirm the original deposit of the gospel message as it was being delivered.

Casting out of demons was part of this confirming work. When Jesus said in Matthew 12:28, *"if I cast out devils by the Spirit of God, then the kingdom of God is come unto you,"* He was making the exorcisms of demons a specific evidence that the kingdom had arrived in His person. They were not ordinary works that any believer would perform throughout the church age. They were a sign that announced the arrival of the Kingdom (the church of Christ) and the authority of the King (Jesus).

The same logic applies to the apostolic exorcisms. When Philip cast out unclean spirits in Samaria (Acts 8:7), or when Paul cast out the spirit of divination from the slave girl in Philippi (Acts 16:18), these were sign works that confirmed the apostolic preaching. They were part of the same confirming activity Hebrews 2:3-4 describes.

The Cessation of the Miraculous

The New Testament also describes the boundary of the miraculous period. Two passages do this work directly.

The first is 1 Corinthians 13:8-10:

> *"Charity never faileth: but whether there be prophecies, they shall fail; whether there be tongues, they shall cease; whether there be knowledge, it shall vanish away. For we know in part, and we prophesy in part. But when that which is perfect is come, then that which is in part shall be done away."*

Paul names three of the miraculous gifts directly: prophecies, tongues, knowledge (in the gift sense, the supernatural impartation of knowledge). He says they will fail, cease, and vanish away. The timing is given as *"when that which is perfect is come."* The perfect is the completed Word of God, the closed canon of Scripture, what Paul calls *"the perfect law of liberty"* in James 1:25 and what we now hold in our hands as the sixty-six books of the Bible. Once the Word was complete, the partial gifts that had served as the means of God's communication during the period of revelation were no longer needed.

The second passage is Ephesians 4:11-13:

> *"And he gave some, apostles; and some, prophets; and some, evangelists; and some, pastors and teachers; For the perfecting of the saints, for the work of the ministry, for the edifying of the body of Christ: Till we all come in the unity of the faith, and of the knowledge of the Son of God, unto a perfect man, unto the measure of the stature of the fulness of Christ."*

Paul names four offices that were given for the building up of the church. Apostles. Prophets. Evangelists. Pastors and teachers. The first two of these belong to the foundational period of the first Century. Ephesians 2:20 confirms it: the church is *"built upon the foundation of the apostles and prophets, Jesus Christ himself being the chief corner stone."* The foundation is laid once. The apostles and prophets did their work. The completed Scripture is the result. Evangelists, pastors, and teachers continue throughout the church age, but the foundational offices that delivered the original revelation are not ongoing.

The miraculous gifts were tied to the apostolic office and to those on whom the apostles laid their hands. Acts 8:14-19 records that the gift of the Holy Spirit in its miraculous manifestation came through the laying on of the apostles' hands. Simon the sorcerer noticed this specifically and offered money to obtain the same ability, which Peter rebuked. The pattern is clear. The miraculous gifts came through apostolic transmission. When the last apostle died, no new transmission could occur. **When the last person who had received the gift through**

apostolic hands died, the active operation of the gifts in the church came to its end.

This is the historical reality the New Testament itself prepared the church for. The miraculous period was not meant to continue indefinitely. It was meant to do its specific work of delivering and confirming the original deposit of the gospel, and then to give way to the era in which the completed Word would be the church's guide.

What This Means for Demon Possession

What does this mean for the dramatic demon possession encounters of the Gospels and Acts?

Those encounters were real. They occurred. The men and women freed from possession by Christ and the apostles were genuinely freed. Scripture is the testimony of that. We do not need to doubt what happened.

But the casting out of demons was part of the same miraculous package as the healings, the tongues, the raising of the dead. It belonged to the period when the kingdom was arriving and the gospel was being established. It was a sign work that confirmed the message. When the apostolic period closed, the demonstration of authority over demons in this dramatic form closed with it.

This does not mean demons stopped existing. Chapter Eight has already established that the hierarchy of fallen beings continues to operate. Chapters Six and Seven have established that the Adversary continues to tempt believers and to accuse them. The Adversary is real. His forces are real. The conflict is real.

What changed at the close of the apostolic period was the manner of the conflict, not its existence. The dramatic possession scenes of the Gospels gave way to the steady spiritual warfare the epistles describe. The believer of the Gadarene's era might have encountered demons in the form Mark 5 describes. The believer of our era encounters the same forces in the form Ephesians 6 describes. The forms differ. The enemy is the same.

The Adversary's primary work today, as Chapters Six and Seven have shown, is temptation, accusation, and the propagation of false doctrine. This is exactly what 1 Timothy 4:1 names as the hierarchy's continued activity in the church age: *"in the latter times some shall depart from the faith, giving heed to seducing spirits, and doctrines of devils."* The mechanism is doctrinal seduction, not dramatic possession. There are no physical demon posessions today. The seducing spirits work through false teachings, false books, false ideas. They do not need to enter and physically control human beings to do their damage. They work at the level of belief and practice, where the damage is more lasting and the operation is harder to recognize.

This is sobering news for the modern believer. The end of dramatic possession does not mean the end of demonic activity. It means the activity has shifted into the form that is harder to detect and easier to spread. A culture that has been emptied of belief in the dramatic supernatural is the perfect culture for the subtler operation. The Adversary does not need theatrical possession in such a setting. He has the field to himself in the realm of ideas, and he is working it without interference from anyone who does not believe he exists.

Four Features of Demon Possession in Mark 5

The Gadarene demoniac story shows several features that appear in other biblical accounts of possession from the period when these events were occurring. These features are useful to know not so we can apply them to modern situations, but so we understand what was happening in the period Scripture describes.

First, supernatural strength. The man could break chains and fetters that ordinary humans could not break. Acts 19:16 shows the same feature. A man with an evil spirit overpowered seven attackers, leaving them naked and wounded. Demon possession in the biblical period sometimes produced physical capabilities that exceeded ordinary human ability.

Second, isolation and association with death. The Gadarene demoniac lived among the tombs. The text emphasizes the location. Tombs are where the dead are. Demonic activity in these accounts drove the afflicted person into isolation, away from human community, and toward associations with death and decay. The Adversary, who was a murderer from the beginning, left his fingerprints on the lives of those he afflicted.

Third, self-destruction. The man cut himself with stones. The boy in Mark 9:22 was cast by the spirit *"into the fire, and into the waters, to destroy him."* Demonic affliction in the biblical period often manifested in self-harm. The Adversary's hatred of human beings, who bear the image of God, expressed itself in destructive activity directed at the very body the demon had invaded.

Fourth, recognition of Christ and submission to His authority. The unclean spirit in Mark 5 recognized Jesus immediately, named Him as the Son of the most high God, and begged not to be tormented. Even in possession, even at the height of demonic activity, the demon knew exactly who Jesus was and was completely subject to His authority. James 2:19 says, *"the devils also believe, and tremble."* Demons have better theology than many human beings. They knew who Christ was. They knew what He had the right to do. They were not in any position to resist His direct command.

These four features, taken together, give a believer a way to read the biblical accounts with understanding. Look at what the four features have in common. Each one is a violation of what God designed the human person to be. Strength turned destructive instead of productive. Community replaced by isolation. The body, made for life, used as an instrument of death. Worship of the Creator replaced by terror of His Son. The Adversary cannot create. He can only spoil. Every feature of demon possession was a corruption of something God made good. That should tell you something about the Adversary's relationship to creation. He hates it because he hates the One who made it. He does to created things what he does because he cannot do anything else.

The Authority of Christ Over Demons in the Biblical Accounts

The pattern of Jesus's encounters with demons in the Gospels is consistent. He commands and they obey. Period. There is no negotiation, no struggle, no protracted contest. The Son of God speaks, and the demonic forces submit.

Mark 1:25 records one of the early encounters: *"And Jesus rebuked him, saying, Hold thy peace, and come out of him."* The unclean spirit obeys immediately. Mark 1:27 reports the response of the watching crowd: *"What thing is this? what new doctrine is this? for with authority commandeth he even the unclean spirits, and they do obey him."* The authority was the noteworthy feature. Other figures in that period had attempted exorcisms. None had done so with this kind of direct, uncontested command.

Jesus delegated this authority to His followers in specific ways during the miraculous period. In Mark 6:7, He sent out the twelve *"and gave them power over unclean spirits."* In Luke 10:17, the seventy returned rejoicing that *"even the devils are subject unto us through thy name."* The authority was real, but it was given in connection with the apostolic mission. It operated through the name (authority) of Jesus during the period when the gospel was being delivered and confirmed.

The book of Acts shows this authority in continued operation through the apostolic period. Philip in Samaria (Acts 8:7). Paul in Philippi (Acts 16:18). Paul cast out the spirit of divination using the formula *"I command thee in the name of Jesus Christ to come out of her."* The authority operated in the name of Christ, through the apostles and those who were part of the apostolic ministry, during the era when these sign works were confirming the apostolic preaching.

The Account of the Sons of Sceva

The story in Acts 19:13-16 deserves a closer look because it shows the boundary of who was authorized to engage demonic forces in the dramatic form, even during the miraculous period.

> *"Then certain of the vagabond Jews, exorcists, took upon them to call over them which had evil spirits the name of the Lord Jesus, saying,*

> *We adjure you by Jesus whom Paul preacheth. And there were seven sons of one Sceva, a Jew, and chief of the priests, which did so. And the evil spirit answered and said, Jesus I know, and Paul I know; but who are ye? And the man in whom the evil spirit was leaped on them, and overcame them, and prevailed against them, so that they fled out of that house naked and wounded."* (Acts 19:13-16)

The seven sons of Sceva were professional exorcists. They had a sort of religious pedigree. They had observed Paul casting out demons in the name of Jesus, and they decided to add the formula to their professional repertoire. They tried it. The demon laughed at them, then he beat them naked.

The episode contains several lessons.

First, the name of Jesus is not a formula. It is the name of a Person. The authority of the name belonged to those whom Christ had specifically commissioned. Outsiders could not borrow the authority. The demon recognized this immediately. He knew Jesus. He knew Paul. He did not know the sons of Sceva, because they were not part of the apostolic mission and had not been commissioned by Christ.

Second, demonic forces have intelligence and discernment. They can tell the difference between someone Christ has authorized and someone trying to use His name without authorization. They are not fooled by religious credentials, family lineage, or professional titles. They look past all of that to whether or not the person is operating under Christ's actual commission.

Third, this episode is one of the few places in Scripture where demonic forces win an immediate physical victory over human beings. The reason they won is that the humans were not actually operating under the authority they claimed. The demon's response was not just to ignore them. It was to attack them physically. This is one of the warnings Scripture gives against trying to engage demonic forces from the wrong position.

The lesson for us is straightforward. The dramatic engagement with demonic forces that happened in the apostolic period was the work of those Christ had specifically authorized. There was no general license to undertake this kind of work. Those who tried it without commission were dealt with severely. The believer today, who lives after the close of the miraculous period, is not commissioned to engage demonic forces in this dramatic form at all. Our commission is different. Our resources are different. Our work is different.

The Believer's Position Today

The closing of the miraculous period does not leave the believer defenseless. It leaves us with what Christ Himself said would be the church's foundation through the centuries: the completed Word of God.

2 Timothy 3:16-17 gives the doctrine of Scripture's sufficiency:

> *"All scripture is given by inspiration of God, and is profitable for doctrine, for reproof, for correction, for instruction in righteousness: That the man of God may be perfect, throughly furnished unto all good works."*

The Word, given by inspiration, is the equipment. It is all-sufficient. It furnishes the believer for **every** good work the Lord has called us to.

Jude 1:3 reinforces the point: the faith was *"once delivered unto the saints."* Once. Not delivered and then re-delivered with each new generation through some form of new revelation. The deposit was made during the apostolic period. The completed Scripture preserves it. The church now contends for what was delivered, rather than waiting for new deliveries.

This is the answer to the question of what the believer does about demonic activity today. We hold to the Word. We test every doctrine against it. We refuse what does not align with it. We walk in obedience to what it commands. We live in dependence on the One the Word reveals. This is the actual front line of spiritual conflict in the present age, because the Adversary's primary work in this age is the corruption of doctrine and the deception of believers.

The New Testament Christian today does not need to look for dramatic encounters with possessing spirits. We do not need to develop techniques of exorcism. We do not need to fear that an evil spirit might enter us or our loved ones. The dramatic possession of the biblical period, with its specific purpose in confirming the apostolic message, is not the form the Adversary's work takes today. His current work is more subtle, and it requires the equipment Scripture has provided: the Word, prayer, the church, and faithfulness in the ordinary obligations of the Christian life.

The Adversary is happy with whatever form gets the work done. In the apostolic age, dramatic possession served his purposes by providing arenas in which Christ's authority would be demonstrated, but only at the cost of him being publicly exposed and defeated. He was willing to absorb those losses because the dramatic encounters were unavoidable in that period. In the present age, he prefers the quieter work that does not require him to be visible. He has been very effective in this work. The number of professing Christians who have been moved off of biblical doctrine by the subtler operations of the Adversary in the last century alone is enormous. The damage has been substantial. And most of it has been done without anyone seeing a demon at all.

What This Means for the Cultural Pictures

The cultural pictures of demon possession can now be put in their proper place.

The horror movie possession is a cultural caricature based loosely on biblical material from the closed apostolic period. It does not describe what is happening in the world today, in the experience of believers or unbelievers. The believer who has absorbed this picture as our primary mental image of demonic activity is looking for the wrong thing.

This does not mean that everyone who has reported strange experiences was lying or imagining things. The mind can be troubled, the conscience can be afflicted, dreams can be disturbed. But none of it warrants the conclusion that dramatic biblical possession is occurring or that special exorcism ministries are needed. The biblical response to spiritual oppression in the post-apostolic period is the same as the biblical response to every other spiritual challenge: the Word, prayer, the church, repentance from any specific sin involved, and the steady resources of the Christian life.

The young believer needs to be protected from the false expectations these cultural pictures create. We do not need to fear that we might be possessed. We do not need to fear that our unbelieving friends might be possessed in any sense that requires special intervention from us. We do not need to be drawn into ministries that promise dramatic encounters with demonic forces. The biblical pattern is steadier, less dramatic, and far more useful for an entire lifetime of walking with Christ.

What Scripture Does Not Teach

A few things should be named that Scripture does not teach about demons today, since these errors are common.

Scripture does not teach that demons reside in physical objects in any way that requires special procedures to remove. The *"haunted object"* of horror tradition is not a biblical category. There are objects associated with occult practices that should not be in a believer's possession (Acts 19:19 records the Ephesian believers burning their books of magic during the apostolic period), but the destruction is about repentance and complete break with the practices, not about exorcising spirits from the books.

Scripture does not teach that specific demons have specific names that the believer needs to know in order to bind them. The "named-demon binding" of some modern ministries is not in the New Testament and certainly is not in any teaching for the post-apostolic age.

Scripture does not teach that generational curses bind believers in a way that requires some form of specific deliverance ministry. Christ has redeemed believers from the curse (Galatians 3:13). The new birth in Christ makes the believer a new creature (2 Corinthians 5:17). Patterns of family sin are real and need to be repented of, but they do not function as binding curses on those who are in Christ.

Scripture does not teach that Christians need to "take authority" over demons in their cities, neighborhoods, or workplaces in elaborate prayer rituals. The biblical pattern, again, is faithfulness, prayer, and the preaching of the Word.

Each of these errors has produced ministries and books and entire teaching traditions. Each of them takes biblical material from the closed apostolic period and stretches it way past anything Scripture authorizes. The believer who holds to what Scripture says, distinguishes the apostolic period from the present age, and refuses what tradition has added will be both more accurate in our understanding and more effective in our actual walk with Christ.

The Modern Occult Landscape

One final matter requires attention. The believer should recognize the modern occult landscape for what it is. The cultural environment around us is full of practices that, while often presented as harmless or as personal "spirituality", are spiritually serious. Tarot cards. Ouija boards. Astrology. Burning incense or sage to clear an old house of bad energy or demons. Crystal healing. New age meditation. Mediums and psychics. None of these is spiritually neutral. Deuteronomy 18:10-12 lists most of them by name and calls them an abomination. The young Christian who keeps their hands off the things Scripture identifies as channels for occult influence, has done a substantial part of the practical work of spiritual self-protection.

This does not mean that anyone who has handled a Ouija board is now possessed by a demon. The dramatic possession of the apostolic period **does not occur today in that way**. But the practices themselves are forbidden, they form spiritual habits that move the practitioner away from God, and they leave the practitioner more open to the Adversary's deceptions in the form they take today. The damage is real even when it does not look like a horror movie.

The cure is also straightforward. Repentance from the practices. Removal of the objects associated with them. A return to walking with God in dependence on His Word. There is no special ritual required. The blood of Christ has covered the sin of the believer who has obeyed Him, and the ordinary practices of the Christian life are the means by which the Spirit of God works the truth of that covering deeper into our experience of daily living.

What This Chapter Establishes

One. Demons are real. The dramatic possession encounters of the Gospels and Acts genuinely occurred during the apostolic period.

Two. Mark 5 and other passages give four features of demon possession in that period: supernatural strength, isolation and association with death, self-destruction, and recognition of and submission to Christ. Each is a corruption of something God made good.

Three. The miraculous works of the apostolic period, including the casting out of demons, served the specific purpose of confirming the gospel as it was first delivered (Hebrews 2:3-4, Mark 16:20).

Four. The miraculous period closed with the apostolic age. 1 Corinthians 13:8-10 and Ephesians 4:11-13 establish that the gifts and offices that operated during that period were not given as ongoing equipment for every generation.

Five. The Adversary's work today is not in the form of dramatic possession but in the subtler forms of temptation, accusation, and the propagation of false doctrine (1 Timothy 4:1).

Six. The believer's equipment for the post-apostolic age is the completed Word of God (2 Timothy 3:16-17), the faith once delivered (Jude 1:3), and the ordinary practices of the Christian life: the Word, prayer, the church, and faithfulness.

Seven. Several common errors should be refused: the haunted object, the named-demon binding, the generational curse on believers, elaborate territorial ritual, and the modern deliverance ministries that assume ongoing dramatic possession. None of these has biblical warrant in the post-apostolic age.

Review Questions

1. Mark 5:1-7 describes the Gadarene demoniac. What four features of demon possession does the chapter identify in this account, and how do they appear in other biblical passages from the apostolic period?

2. The chapter says the Gospels distinguish between demonic affliction and physical or mental illness, citing Matthew 4:24 and Mark 1:32-34. Why is this distinction important for how a believer reads the biblical accounts?

3. Hebrews 2:3-4 says the miraculous works *"confirmed"* the message that was first spoken by the Lord. What was the purpose of the miraculous works in the apostolic period, and how does this purpose shape how we read the casting out of demons?

4. 1 Corinthians 13:8-10 says prophecies, tongues, and knowledge will fail, cease, and vanish away *"when that which is perfect is come."* What is the perfect, and how does this passage establish the boundary of the miraculous period?

5. Ephesians 4:11-13 names four offices given to the church. Which two belong to the foundational period, and how does Ephesians 2:20 confirm this reading?

6. Acts 8:14-19 records that miraculous gifts came through the laying on of the apostles' hands. What does this transmission pattern tell us about why the miraculous gifts ceased after the apostolic period?

7. The chapter says the Adversary's work today is *"not in the form of dramatic possession but in the subtler forms of temptation, accusation, and the propagation of false doctrine."* How does 1 Timothy 4:1 describe the form of demonic activity that continues in the church age?

8. The chapter argues that the modern world is the perfect environment for the subtler operations of the Adversary, because a culture that does not believe in the dramatic supernatural will not recognize the quieter work either. How does this observation explain why the church has lost so much doctrinal ground in recent generations?

9. The chapter identifies four features of demon possession that all share something in common: each is a corruption of something God made good. How does this insight reveal the Adversary's relationship to creation?

10. James 2:19 says *"the devils also believe, and tremble."* What does this verse tell us about demonic theology compared to human theology?

11. The seven sons of Sceva in Acts 19 tried to use the name of Jesus without authorization, and the demon attacked them. What does this episode establish about who was authorized to engage demonic forces in the apostolic period, and what does it imply for the present?

12. 2 Timothy 3:16-17 says Scripture furnishes the believer "throughly...unto all good works." How does this verse address the question of whether the believer in the post-apostolic age lacks anything we need for spiritual conflict?

13. Jude 1:3 says the faith was *"once delivered unto the saints."* How does this single past delivery shape the way the church relates to claims of new revelation or new patterns of supernatural ministry?

14. The chapter identifies four common errors that Scripture does not teach today: the haunted object, the named-demon binding, the generational curse on believers, and elaborate territorial ritual, along with modern deliverance ministries that assume ongoing dramatic possession. Why is the cessationist position on the miraculous period the safeguard against each of these errors?

15. Deuteronomy 18:10-12 lists occult practices and calls them an abomination. The chapter applies this to modern practices like tarot, Ouija boards, astrology, and mediums. Why is dabbling in these spiritually serious even though dramatic biblical possession does not occur today?

REFERENCES

1. On the Gadarene demoniac in Mark 5 and the features of demonic possession in the Gospels, see R. T. France, The Gospel of Mark, New International Greek Testament Commentary (Grand Rapids: Eerdmans, 2002).

2. On the distinction between demonic affliction and physical illness in the New Testament, see Graham H. Twelftree, Jesus the Exorcist: A Contribution to the Study of the Historical Jesus (Tubingen: J.C.B. Mohr, 1993).

3. On the cessation of miraculous gifts and the closing of the apostolic period, see Richard B. Gaffin Jr., Perspectives on Pentecost: New Testament Teaching on the Gifts of the Holy Spirit (Phillipsburg: Presbyterian and Reformed, 1979).

4. On 1 Corinthians 13:8-10 and the meaning of *"that which is perfect,"* see Robert L. Reymond, A New Systematic Theology of the Christian Faith, second edition (Nashville: Thomas Nelson, 1998).

5. On Ephesians 4:11-13 and the apostolic foundation of the church, see Andrew T. Lincoln, Ephesians, Word Biblical Commentary (Dallas: Word Books, 1990).

6. On Acts 8:14-19 and the apostolic transmission of miraculous gifts, see F. F. Bruce, The Book of Acts, New International Commentary on the New Testament (Grand Rapids: Eerdmans, 1988).

7. On the dangers of common errors in modern deliverance ministries from a cessationist perspective, see John MacArthur, Strange Fire: The Danger of Offending the Holy Spirit with Counterfeit Worship (Nashville: Thomas Nelson, 2013).

8. On Hebrews 2:3-4 and the confirming purpose of the miraculous, see Philip Edgcumbe Hughes, A Commentary on the Epistle to the Hebrews (Grand Rapids: Eerdmans, 1977).

CHAPTER TEN

What Satan Cannot Do

"And the LORD said unto Satan, Hast thou considered my servant Job, that there is none like him in the earth, a perfect and an upright man, one that feareth God, and escheweth evil? Then Satan answered the LORD, and said, Doth Job fear God for nought? Hast not thou made an hedge about him, and about his house, and about all that he hath on every side? thou hast blessed the work of his hands, and his substance is increased in the land. But put forth thine hand now, and touch all that he hath, and he will curse thee to thy face. And the LORD said unto Satan, Behold, all that he hath is in thy power; only upon himself put not forth thine hand. So Satan went forth from the presence of the LORD." (Job 1:8-12)

The conversation between God and Satan in Job 1 is the most direct biblical statement of the limits the Adversary operates under. Satan can act against Job. But only within boundaries the Lord has set. He can touch Job's possessions. He cannot touch Job's body. Later, in chapter 2, the Lord extends the permission to Job's body but specifies that his life cannot be taken. The Adversary operates within a fence the Lord has built, and the fence is real.

The previous chapter took up what demons did in the first century and what they don't do today. This chapter takes up what the Adversary cannot do. His limits are as important to understand as his abilities, because both belong to the biblical picture, and the Christian who knows only what the Devil can do, without knowing what he cannot do, will live in disproportionate fear.

A young believer needs to feel the practical importance of this chapter. The Adversary has a great interest in being thought of as more powerful than he is. The bigger he can make himself look, the more paralyzed his targets become. The biblical picture is the correction. He is real. He is dangerous. He is also bounded. He cannot do most of what people fear he can do. He cannot do anything God has not permitted. The fence is real, and you are inside it.

The Permission Structure

The Job 1 conversation establishes a principle that runs throughout Scripture. Satan operates by permission, not by independent authority. He must request access. The request can be granted or denied. The terms of the access are set by God, not by Satan.

Luke 22:31 confirms the principle: *"Simon, Simon, behold, Satan hath desired to have you, that he may sift you as wheat."* The verb suggests Satan asked permission. Jesus's response, *"But I have prayed for thee, that thy faith fail not,"* shows that the Lord's response to the request was specific intercession on Peter's behalf.

This is the situation under which the Adversary operates against every believer. He may request access. The request goes through a court that has the believer's interests in mind. When access is granted, it is granted with limits. The limits are not negotiable by him. They are set by the One who knows exactly what the believer can bear and what we need in order to grow.

1 Corinthians 10:13 names the principle from the believer's side:

> *"There hath no temptation taken you but such as is common to man: but God is faithful, who will not suffer you to be tempted above that ye are able; but will with the temptation also make a way to escape, that ye may be able to bear it."*

Look at what this verse promises. The temptations the believer faces are common, not unique. God is faithful, which is the foundation under everything else. He will not suffer the temptation to exceed what the believer can bear. He will provide a way of escape with every temptation. The fence is built into every situation. The believer's job is to look for the door God has provided rather than to be fixated on the wall the Adversary has erected.

Not Omnipresent

God is everywhere. The Adversary is not. He is a created being, located in space, present in one place at a time. He cannot be in your bedroom and on the other side of the world simultaneously. The vast majority of his work in the world is done not by him personally but his influence spread by humans everywhere.

This is more practically important than it first sounds. Many believers carry a low-level dread that the Devil is constantly watching them, evaluating them, working against them personally. **He is not.** He is one creature among many. He cannot be in every Christian's life at every moment.

This does not minimize the seriousness of the conflict. His influence is still very real, still organized, still capable of significant damage. But it does correct a picture that has paralyzed believers needlessly. The young Christian who imagines that our every step is being personally observed by Satan himself can let that picture go. He is not watching our every move. He may not be aware of us at all. The forces that oppose us in our actual life are part of his organization, but they are not him.

Compare this to God. God is omnipresent. Psalm 139 makes this explicit.

> *"To the chief Musician, A Psalm of David. O LORD, thou hast searched me, and known me. Thou knowest my downsitting and mine uprising, thou understandest my thought afar off. Thou compassest my path and my lying down, and art acquainted with all my ways. For there is not a word in my tongue, but, lo, O LORD, thou*

> *knowest it altogether. Thou hast beset me behind and before, and laid thine hand upon me. Such knowledge is too wonderful for me; it is high, I cannot attain unto it. Whither shall I go from thy spirit? or whither shall I flee from thy presence? If I ascend up into heaven, thou art there: if I make my bed in hell, behold, thou art there. If I take the wings of the morning, and dwell in the uttermost parts of the sea; Even there shall thy hand lead me, and thy right hand shall hold me. If I say, Surely the darkness shall cover me; even the night shall be light about me. Yea, the darkness hideth not from thee; but the night shineth as the day: the darkness and the light are both alike to thee. For thou hast possessed my reins: thou hast covered me in my mother's womb. I will praise thee; for I am fearfully and wonderfully made: marvellous are thy works; and that my soul knoweth right well. My substance was not hid from thee, when I was made in secret, and curiously wrought in the lowest parts of the earth. Thine eyes did see my substance, yet being unperfect; and in thy book all my members were written, which in continuance were fashioned, when as yet there was none of them. How precious also are thy thoughts unto me, O God! how great is the sum of them! If I should count them, they are more in number than the sand: when I awake, I am still with thee. Surely thou wilt slay the wicked, O God: depart from me therefore, ye bloody men. For they speak against thee wickedly, and thine enemies take thy name in vain. Do not I hate them, O LORD, that hate thee? and am not I grieved with those that rise up against thee? I hate them with perfect hatred: I count them mine enemies. Search me, O God, and know my heart: try me, and know my thoughts: And see if there be any wicked way in me, and lead me in the way everlasting."* (Psalms 139:1-24)

There is no place a believer can go where God is not. There is no moment in which God is not aware of us. There is no situation in which the Lord is not present with us in the fullest possible sense. The contrast is total. God's presence is everywhere with the believer. The Adversary's presence is somewhere, perhaps not where we are. The asymmetry is not subtle. It is fundamental.

Not Omniscient

God knows all things. The Adversary does not. He has intelligence, observation, and accumulated experience. He can read external behaviors, words, and patterns. He can make educated inferences about what is going on inside a person.

But he cannot read the heart directly. 1 Kings 8:39 attributes that ability to God alone: *"for thou, even thou only, knowest the hearts of all the children of men."* Jeremiah 17:10 makes the same claim:

> *"I the LORD search the heart, I try the reins, even to give every man according to his ways, and according to the fruit of his doings."*

God's knowledge of man's heart is one of God's exclusive attributes.

This means the Adversary works largely from what is observable on the outside. He hears what you say. He sees what you do. He notices the patterns in your life over time, including the patterns in your external (said out-loud) prayer life, your Bible reading, your relationships. He builds profiles based on observation. But the secret prayer in the closet, the silent thought of love for God, the inner repentance that does not yet show on the outside, are closed to him.

This is enormously important for the believer's prayer life. The intercession that goes on between you and God in private is genuinely private. The Adversary cannot eavesdrop on it directly. He may notice that you are spending time alone or that you appear changed afterward, but the actual content of your communion with God is between you and God. He has no access to it. The treasure that you store up in heaven through faithful unseen obedience is hidden from him in the same way it is hidden from human observers, only more so.

This also has implications for spiritual battle. The Adversary's strategies are based on partial information. He guesses at your weak points based on what he can observe. He guesses wrong sometimes. The believer who walks consistently with God presents a target that is harder for him to read accurately, because the visible signs of our lives are less correlated with the inner condition of our hearts. The Adversary loses one of his major tactical advantages over a believer who has been deeply hidden in Christ.

Not Omnipotent

God can do all things. The Adversary cannot. He has significant power, but his power is bounded by his nature as a creature and by the permissions the Lord grants or denies him.

The Job narrative shows this directly. He could not act against Job's possessions until permitted. He could not act against Job's body until permitted. He could not take Job's life because that permission was not granted. The boundaries were not negotiated by Satan. They were set by God and observed.

Hebrews 1:14 reminds us that the holy angels are sent forth to minister to those who shall be heirs of salvation. The fallen angels operate against the same heirs of salvation. There is asymmetry in the comparison. The holy angels are vastly more numerous (two-thirds remained faithful, by the Revelation 12 calculation), they are operating with the full power of God behind them, and they are deployed to protect and serve the people of God. The fallen angels are smaller in number, operating within constraints, and matched at every point by the angelic forces that oppose them.

The Adversary's power is also derivative. He has no original power. Every capability he possesses was given to him as a created being and was not removed from him at the fall. He still has the abilities of a high-order created being. He cannot exceed those abilities. He cannot create matter. He cannot raise the dead. He cannot read hearts. He cannot grant eternal life. He cannot save anyone. He cannot alter the basic structure of reality. He can only operate within the structure that God created, using the abilities God gave him, within the permissions God grants in any given situation.

Not Autonomous

This brings us to the biggest limit of all. The Adversary is not autonomous. He cannot do anything God has not permitted. Every move he makes is, in the end, a move that God has allowed.

> This raises hard questions about the relationship between God's sovereignty and the existence of evil, questions that have produced a lot of bad theology over the centuries. The biblical answer is not that God authors evil. James 1:13 is explicit:

> *"Let no man say when he is tempted, I am tempted of God: for God cannot be tempted with evil, neither tempteth he any man."*

God does not tempt. God does not author the Adversary's evil purposes.

But God does superintend. He sets the boundaries. He decides what permissions to grant. He uses the Adversary's evil intentions to accomplish His own good purposes, as Genesis 50:20 says of Joseph's brothers:

> *"But as for you, ye thought evil against me; but God meant it unto good."*

The Adversary intends harm. God uses the harm to bring about something he never intended. The Adversary cannot escape this superintendence. Even his deepest rebellion serves God's eternal plan in the end.

This is why the believer can endure Adversary's attacks without ultimate loss. The harm he intends is real. The harm we suffer is real. But the outcome is in God's hands, and God uses even the Adversary's worst work to bring about the believer's good and His own glory. Romans 8:28 is the great statement:

> *"And we know that all things work together for good to them that love God, to them who are the called according to his purpose."*

Even the Adversary's attacks are among the "*all things*." Even those work together for good. The Adversary cannot prevent this. He cannot derail it. He cannot win against it.

Zoroastrian Dualism Is Not Biblical

A common misconception is that good and evil are roughly equivalent forces locked in cosmic combat with the outcome uncertain. This is the framework of Zoroastrian dualism, which has influenced Western thought through various channels but has nothing to do with biblical theology.

In Scripture, God is infinite, eternal, and uncreated. The Adversary is finite, created, and limited in every dimension. They are not opposing forces of equal weight. They are Creator and creature. The contest is not in doubt. It has never been in doubt. Revelation 20:10 announces the final outcome with no ambiguity:

> *"And the devil that deceived them was cast into the lake of fire and brimstone, where the beast and the false prophet are, and shall be tormented day and night for ever and ever."*

The cosmic conflict is real, but it is not symmetrical. The Lord allows the Adversary to operate within boundaries for purposes that include the testing and refining of His people, the displaying of His glory in the midst of opposition, and the demonstration that even the worst evil cannot derail His good purposes. The

Adversary's eventual defeat is not in question. The only question is what the Lord will do through this period of permitted operation before the final judgment.

A young Christian who has absorbed dualism, even unconsciously, will think about our own struggles in a wrong way. They will think the outcome of our individual battles is uncertain. We will think the Adversary might actually win against us. We will be tempted to despair when we see evil seem to triumph in some specific situation. The correction to this is to remember the asymmetry. God is God. The Adversary is a creature. The contest, on the macro scale, is decided. The contest, in our individual life, is supervised by the Lord who **has** built a fence around us. We may suffer real losses inside that fence. We cannot lose in any final sense. The Lord has guaranteed our ultimate good as part of the all things that work together if we love and serve Him alone.

The Difference Between Power and Authority

A useful distinction to make at this point is the difference between power and authority. The Adversary has power. He has been a high-order created being since before the human race existed, and he retains substantial capability. But power and authority are not the same thing.

Authority is the right to use power. A police officer has authority. A criminal with a weapon may have more raw power than the officer in a particular moment. But the officer has the right to use power on behalf of the law. The criminal does not. The contest, when fully played out, is decided by authority, not by raw capability in the moment.

The Adversary lost his authority at the fall. He retained his powers as a created being, but his right to exercise those powers in service of God's purposes was forfeited. He now operates as a rebel. His powers are real but they are exercised illegitimately, against the One who originally gave them.

In extreme contrast to Satan, Christ has **all** authority. Matthew 28:18 records His statement after the resurrection: *"All power is given unto me in heaven and in earth."* The word translated *"power"* in the King James is the Greek *exousia*, which means authority. All authority. In heaven and on earth. There is no jurisdiction outside His authority. There is no situation His authority does not cover.

The obedient believer in Christ operates under His authority. We are not exercising our own power. We are acting on the authority of the One whose authority is total. The Adversary may have raw power in some encounter with us. The contest is not decided by the comparison of powers. It is decided by the comparison of authorities. It is grounded in the One who has all authority. His was forfeited at the fall.

This is why Jesus could send the seventy out with the assurance that "*the devils are subject unto you through my name*" (Luke 10:17). The disciples did not just have more raw power than the demons they encountered. They had authority that the demons did not have, because they had Christ. The same is true of the believer today. We do not need to match the Adversary's power. We need to subject ourselves to living in and under Christ's authority. Authority decides the contest.

How God Uses the Adversary's Worst Work

One of the more startling truths in Scripture is that God uses even the Adversary's most destructive work to accomplish purposes the Adversary did not intend. The cross itself is the supreme example. Acts 2:23 says of Jesus: "

> *Him, being delivered by the determinate counsel and foreknowledge of God, ye have taken, and by wicked hands have crucified and slain."*

The crucifixion was both the worst evil ever committed and the central act of God's plan of salvation. The Adversary's deepest move against Christ became the means of his own defeat!

This pattern continues in the lives of the followers of Jesus. The persecution of the early church scattered believers across the Roman Empire (Acts 8:4) and accelerated the spread of the gospel. The death of martyrs throughout history has produced more conversions, not fewer. The hardships individual Christians have suffered at the Adversary's instigation have, in case after case, become the very experiences that made them most useful in ministry.

This does not mean evil is good. Evil is evil. It always will be. The Adversary's intentions are wicked. The harm he causes is real harm, and the suffering it produces is real suffering. But the Lord's superintendence is total. He uses what the Adversary intended for evil to accomplish good that the Adversary cannot prevent.

The Christian who internalizes this can live without the kind of paralyzing fear of the future that the Adversary likes to cultivate. Whatever happens, the Lord will use it. **The Adversary cannot bring about a situation that the Lord cannot turn to good.** Read that again and do so slowly. He cannot construct a defeat that the Lord cannot reverse. He cannot inflict a wound that the Lord cannot heal, or use, or both. The believer's confidence is not in the absence of the Adversary's attacks. It is in the presence of the Lord who superintends them.

The Final End: Revelation 20

Revelation 20:7-10 describes the Adversary's final career and final end. After being released from his binding for a final time, he gathers his forces, surrounds the camp of the saints, and is consumed by fire from heaven. Then:

> *"And the devil that deceived them was cast into the lake of fire and brimstone, where the beast and the false prophet are, and shall be tormented day and night for ever and ever."* (Revelation 20:10)

This is the path that the Adversary has been on since his fall. Every move he makes is a move toward this end. Every act of opposition against God's people is also another step in his own self-destruction. He cannot stop the trajectory. He cannot escape the destination. He has known where he is going since the moment of his fall, and he is going there as surely as time is moving.

For the Christian, this is some extremely settling news. Every conflict we face with the Adversary is a conflict with a defeated being on his way to a settled end. The conflict feels real because it is real, but the outcome is not in doubt. The Adversary cannot win against the believer who is in Christ, because the Adversary cannot win against Christ, and the believer is hidden in Christ. The Adversary is fighting a battle he cannot win, on a trajectory he cannot change, against an opponent he cannot defeat. The believer who internalizes this stops being intimidated by him because we know something vitally important – we win and he loses. Period. Full Stop.

The Limits in Practical Terms

Pull all of these limits together for the practical use of the believer.

The Adversary can attack you, but only by permission, and only within limits the Lord has set in your specific case.

He can read your behavior, but not your heart. The deepest things between you and God are out of his reach.

He can be in only one place at a time. He cannot be personally focused on you in the moment you imagine. The opposition you face is most often the work of his subordinates, not him personally.

He can do only what created beings can do, within the further limit of what God permits him to do. He cannot exceed the powers God gave him, and he cannot exceed the permissions God grants him.

He cannot escape the trajectory God has set for him. Every move he makes is a move toward the lake of fire. He cannot prevent his end. He cannot delay it past the appointed time.

He cannot win against you in any final sense. The Lord uses even his worst attacks to bring about your good. The Adversary cannot derail this. He cannot prevent the all things from working together for your good.

These limits are real. The believer who knows them stops being paralyzed by an Adversary who is not nearly as strong as we thought he was. We can take him seriously without giving him more credit than Scripture gives him. We can resist him without panic. We can stand against him without despair. The fence is real. We are inside it. The One who built it is on the throne, and the One who is on the throne is for us.

What This Chapter Establishes

One. The Adversary operates by permission, not by independent authority. He must request access, and the request goes through a court that supervises his every move.

Two. He is not omnipresent. He is a created being, located in space, present in only one place at a time. Most of the opposition believers face is the work of subordinate demonic beings, not the personal attention of Satan himself.

Three. He is not omniscient. He works from observable behaviors and patterns. The heart is closed to him. Private prayer and silent inner devotion are out of his reach.

Four. He is not omnipotent. His powers are derivative, bounded by the abilities of a created being and by the permissions God grants in any given situation.

Five. He is not autonomous. Every move he makes is a move God has permitted. God uses his evil intentions to accomplish good purposes the Adversary never intended.

Six. Zoroastrian dualism is not biblical. The contest between God and Satan is not symmetrical. God is Creator. Satan is creature. The outcome is settled.

Seven. Revelation 20:10 announces the Adversary's final end. He is on a trajectory toward the lake of fire. He cannot escape it.

Review Questions

1. Job 1:8-12 shows God setting specific boundaries for what Satan can and cannot do to Job. What does this passage establish about the permission structure under which the Adversary operates?

2. Luke 22:31 says Satan *"desired"* to have Peter, suggesting he asked permission. How does Jesus's response change the situation, and what does this pattern tell us about Adversary's access to believers?

3. 1 Corinthians 10:13 promises that God will not allow temptation to exceed what a believer can bear, and that He will provide a way of escape. How does this verse affect the way a believer should think about us difficulties?

4. The chapter says the Adversary is not omnipresent, that he is one creature in one place at a time, and that most opposition believers face is the work of his subordinates. How does this picture correct the common dread that "the Devil is watching me personally"?

5. The chapter contrasts the Adversary's local presence with God's omnipresence. How does Psalm 139's affirmation of God's universal presence apply to a believer's daily life?

6. 1 Kings 8:39 and Jeremiah 17:10 attribute heart-knowledge to God alone. What are the implications for the Adversary's tactical knowledge of believers?

7. The chapter says private prayer is genuinely private from the Adversary's perspective. How does this affect the way a believer should value our hidden devotional life?

8. The chapter argues that a believer who walks consistently with God presents a target the Adversary cannot read accurately. How does deep hiddenness in Christ work as a tactical advantage?

9. Job 1 and 2 show that the Adversary's power was bounded by specific permissions. What were those permissions, and what does it mean that God set them rather than Satan?

10. Hebrews 1:14 reminds us that holy angels minister to *"the heirs of salvation."* How does the asymmetry between holy and fallen angels affect how a believer should think about spiritual conflict?

11. James 1:13 says God does not tempt anyone. Genesis 50:20 says God uses evil intentions to bring about good purposes. How do these verses together describe the relationship between God's sovereignty and the Adversary's evil?

12. Romans 8:28 says all things work together for good for those who love God. How does this verse apply specifically to the Adversary's attacks against believers?

13. The chapter argues that Zoroastrian dualism, the framework of two roughly equal cosmic forces, is not biblical. What is the biblical alternative, and how does it change a believer's outlook in difficult moments?

14. Revelation 20:10 announces the Adversary's final destination in the lake of fire. How does knowing the final outcome change the believer's posture in present conflicts?

15. The chapter ends with seven specific limits on the Adversary's power. Walk through each one and explain how it changes the believer's daily relationship to spiritual conflict.

REFERENCES

1. On Job 1-2 and the permission structure of the Adversary's operations, see John E. Hartley, The Book of Job, New International Commentary on the Old Testament (Grand Rapids: Eerdmans, 1988).

2. On 1 Corinthians 10:13 and the way of escape, see Gordon D. Fee, The First Epistle to the Corinthians, New International Commentary on the New Testament (Grand Rapids: Eerdmans, 1987).

3. On the limits of demonic knowledge and power, see Sydney H. T. Page, Powers of Evil: A Biblical Study of Satan and Demons (Grand Rapids: Baker, 1995).

4. On the relationship between God's sovereignty and the existence of evil, see John S. Feinberg, The Many Faces of Evil: Theological Systems and the Problems of Evil (Wheaton: Crossway, 2004).

5. On Zoroastrian dualism and its incompatibility with biblical theology, see Mary Boyce, Zoroastrians: Their Religious Beliefs and Practices (London: Routledge, 2001), with biblical critique in D. A. Carson, How Long, O Lord? Reflections on Suffering and Evil (Grand Rapids: Baker, 1990).

6. On Revelation 20 and the final defeat of the Adversary, see G. K. Beale, The Book of Revelation, New International Greek Testament Commentary (Grand Rapids: Eerdmans, 1999).

CHAPTER ELEVEN

Satan Has Already Been Defeated

"And I will put enmity between thee and the woman, and between thy seed and her seed; it shall bruise thy head, and thou shalt bruise his heel." (Genesis 3:15)

The first prophecy in the Bible is also the first announcement of the Adversary's defeat. God speaks these words to the Serpent in the garden, immediately after the Fall. **There will be enmity.** There will be a Seed of the woman. The Seed will bruise the Serpent's head. The Serpent will bruise the Seed's heel.

This passage is sometimes called the *protoevangelium*, the first gospel. It is the seed promise from which the rest of scripture grows. The Adversary's defeat was announced before the human race had even been expelled from the garden. The whole story that follows is the story of how that announcement was carried out, leading to the cross, the empty tomb, and the lake of fire.

The previous chapter showed you what the Adversary cannot do. This chapter takes up what has already been done about him. He is not just limited. He is defeated. Not in the future. Already. The decisive battle was fought at Calvary and the verdict was returned at the empty tomb. Everything since then is the working out of a settled outcome.

Every Christian needs to feel the weight of this chapter. The whole tone of the Christian life changes when we understand that we are not fighting for victory. We are fighting from victory. The Adversary is not a possible threat to our ultimate good. He is a defeated being whose remaining activity is the convulsions of the doomed. The Lord has settled the case. We live, pray, and resist in the assurance that what has already been won will, on the appointed day, be made fully visible.

The *Protoevangelium*

Genesis 3:15 is short, packed, and decisive. Let's briefly look at each part.

"And I will put enmity between thee and the woman." The opposition between the Serpent and humanity is not original to humanity. It is established by God Himself. From this verse forward, the human race will not be at peace with the Serpent. There will be a contest. The Lord has set the terms.

"And between thy seed and her seed." The contest is generational. The Serpent's seed are those who continue in his rebellion. The woman's seed includes all who, by faith, will be aligned against the Serpent. There is a particular Seed, singular, who will be the decisive figure. Galatians 3:16 confirms this reading:

> *"Now to Abraham and his seed were the promises made. He saith not, And to seeds, as of many; but as of one, And to thy seed, which is Christ."*

"It shall bruise thy head." The blow to the head is fatal. The Serpent will be struck where the strike is decisive. This is the announcement of the cross before the cross. The Lord told the Serpent on the day of the Fall that the day of his crushing was coming.

"And thou shalt bruise his heel." The Serpent's strike will reach the Seed but only to the heel, not to the head. The Serpent will wound. He will not destroy. The wound to the heel is real. The strike to the head is final.

The asymmetry in the prophecy is the asymmetry of the cross. Christ was wounded. He was killed. He was buried. But the wound was to the heel, not to the head. He rose. The Serpent has not. The contest's geometry was named in the garden. The geometry held all the way to Calvary and through to the empty tomb.

This passage gives a young believer something to keep in our heads about the whole impact of biblical history. The Bible is not a collection of unrelated stories. It is one story, with a single plot, that runs from the announcement in Genesis 3:15 to the fulfillment in Revelation 20:10. Every story in between is part of the working out of this one plot. The Lord said He would crush the Serpent's head. He has been doing it ever since. He is doing it right now. He will finish it on the day He has appointed.

Colossians 2:13-15 and the Triumphal Procession

Paul gives one of the most vivid descriptions of the cross's effect on the principalities and powers in Colossians 2:13-15:

> *"And you, being dead in your sins and the uncircumcision of your flesh, hath he quickened together with him, having forgiven you all trespasses; Blotting out the handwriting of ordinances that was against us, which was contrary to us, and took it out of the way, nailing it to his cross; And having spoiled principalities and powers, he made a shew of them openly, triumphing over them in it."*

The image is of a Roman triumphal procession. When a Roman general won a major military victory, he was granted a triumph. The triumph was a public parade through Rome. The general rode in a chariot. His troops marched behind him. The captured enemies, stripped of their weapons and their dignity, were dragged through the streets in chains. The crowds saw the defeated enemies in their humiliation. The general's victory was made public.

Paul applies this image to Christ at the cross. The principalities and powers, the same hierarchies named in Ephesians 6:12, were *"spoiled,"* meaning stripped, disarmed, plundered. Christ *"made a shew of them openly,"* meaning He paraded them in their defeat. He *"triumphed over them in it,"* meaning the cross was the chariot of His triumph and the moment of their public humiliation.

The picture reframes everything. The cross looks like the Adversary's victory. Jesus is dead. His followers have scattered. The Roman authorities and the religious authorities have done their worst. The Adversary appears to have won. But Paul says the opposite is happening, even at the moment it appears the Adversary has succeeded. The cross is the Roman triumph in reverse. The principalities and powers, who thought they were the conquerors, are actually being marched in chains behind the chariot of the One they thought they had defeated.

This means that every subsequent encounter the believer has with the principalities and powers is an encounter with a defeated enemy. The hierarchy is real, but it has been disarmed. The leaders of the rebellion are not figures whose victory is still possible. They are prisoners whose defeat was made public at the cross and whose final disposition is fixed.

A faithful believer who internalizes this, fights differently. We do not approach spiritual conflict wondering if we will win. We approach it knowing we are on the side that has already won. Our resistance is not the desperate stand of a soldier in a losing army. It is the standard work of a soldier in an occupying army that has already established its victory and is now mopping up the resistance. The tone is completely different. So is the outcome.

Hebrews 2:14-15 and the Power of Death

The book of Hebrews provides another statement of what the cross accomplished against the Adversary. Hebrews 2:14-15:

> *"Forasmuch then as the children are partakers of flesh and blood, he also himself likewise took part of the same; that through death he*

> *might destroy him that had the power of death, that is, the devil; And deliver them who through fear of death were all their lifetime subject to bondage."*

Several details require attention.

First, the cross is described as the means by which Christ destroyed the one who had the power of death. The Greek verb translated *"destroy"* here is *katargeo*, meaning to render ineffective, to nullify, to bring to nothing. The same verb is used elsewhere for the abolishing of the law's condemning function (Romans 3:31, Galatians 3:17, with related forms). The Adversary's power of death has been nullified. Not delayed. Nullified.

Second, the means of destruction was Christ's own death. This is the strategic genius of the cross. The Adversary held the power of death over humanity. Christ took on flesh and blood, died, and through dying broke the power of the one whose primary leverage was death. The weapon the Adversary used to bind humanity was used against him. Death, his tool, became the means of his defeat.

Third, the result for believers is deliverance "from fear of death." The bondage Hebrews names is not just the fact of mortality. It is the fear that runs underneath every human life. The Adversary uses the fear of death to push and pull human beings into countless wrong decisions. Take the easier path because life is short. Get what you want now because you may not get another chance. Compromise the truth because standing for it might cost you. The fear of death runs underneath all of these. The cross has cut the connection. Death no longer has the same leverage. The believer who is no longer afraid of death is harder to manipulate by every fear that flowed from death.

A young believer can think about this very practically. The Adversary's leverage on us decisions, much of the time, is some version of "but you might lose something" if you obey. The full and final form of "you might lose something" is "you might die." The cross has answered the death question. If even death has been overcome by Christ, the smaller losses do not have the leverage they would otherwise have.

The believer who is settled about death is settled about everything that flows from death. The Adversary has lost his largest tool against us.

1 John 3:8 and the Destruction of His Works

> *"He that committeth sin is of the devil; for the devil sinneth from the beginning. For this purpose the Son of God was manifested, that he might destroy the works of the devil."* (1 John 3:8)

John names the purpose of the incarnation of Jesus in direct terms. The Son of God was manifested in the flesh to destroy the Adversary's works. The Greek verb here for the word "destroy" is *luo*, meaning to loose, to release, to destroy what has been bound together. The Adversary has built up a body of work in the world, a network of effects, a pattern of damage. The Son came to take it dismantle and destroy it.

This is happening continuously through our time. Every time a sinner is converted, the Adversary's work in that life is being destroyed. Every time a marriage that was being torn apart by sin is restored through repentance and forgiveness, the Adversary's work is being destroyed. Every time a captive of addiction is freed by the gospel, the Adversary's work is being destroyed. Every time a child of believing parents is brought up in the faith and stands firm in adulthood, the Adversary's work is being destroyed. The work is not finished. It is in continuous progress. Christ is dismantling, person by person, situation by situation, what the Adversary has built.

Every Christian participates in this work. When we share the gospel, we are part of the destruction of the Adversary's works. When we live faithfully and resists temptation, we are part of the destruction. When we serve the church and loves our brothers and sisters, we are part of the destruction. The project of dismantling the Adversary's work has thousands of human hands attached to it, and our hands are among them.

The Already and the Not Yet

The Adversary has been defeated. He is also still active. Both of these are true. The pattern in the New Testament is sometimes called the "already and not yet" of Christ's work.

The cross has accomplished the decisive victory. The Adversary has been defeated. The principalities and powers have been spoiled. The power of death has been broken. The works of the Devil are being destroyed.

At the same time, the full visible manifestation of this victory is still to come. The Adversary still has limited operations. He still tempts. He still accuses. He still deceives. His final removal from the field has not yet happened.

The believer lives in the gap between these two. We walk in a victory that has been won but is not yet fully manifest. We do not need to win the war, because the war is won. We do not yet see the full visible cessation of opposition, because the day of this full manifestation is still ahead.

This is why Scripture commands the believer to "stand" rather than to "advance" in Ephesians 6:11-13. Standing assumes ground already taken. The believer is not fighting to capture territory. We are holding territory that has already been captured by Christ. Our resistance has the character of an occupying force, not an invading one.

This is also why Scripture is full of confidence in tone, even though the conflict is real. Romans 8:37 says *"we are more than conquerors through him that loved us."* The word "conquerers" is the Greek word *hupernikao*, meaning to over-conquer, to win beyond winning. The believer is described not just as a winner but as a super-winner. The exaggeration is intentional. It captures the unequal nature of a battle where the believer's side has already won the central war and is now collecting the scattered remnants of opposition. The metaphor of being *"more than conquerors"* only makes sense if the conquering is no longer in doubt.

A faithful Christian who has caught this tone fights differently. We do not panic. We do not despair. We do not wonder if we have been abandoned. We know what is happening. We have been placed in an occupied territory whose ultimate liberation is settled. Our job is to hold ground, share the gospel with the population, and wait for the Commander to return. He is coming. The mop-up is finite.

Revelation 20:10 and the End

The final defeat of the Adversary is described in Revelation 20:10:

> *"And the devil that deceived them was cast into the lake of fire and brimstone, where the beast and the false prophet are, and shall be tormented day and night for ever and ever."*

This is the destination toward which the Adversary has been moving since his fall. Every act of opposition against God and against God's people is also a step in his own progress toward this end. He cannot escape it. He cannot delay it past the time appointed. He cannot negotiate it. He will be cast into the lake of fire, and his torment will be without end.

This is hard reading for a sentimental modern reader. But it is what Scripture says, and it has implications for the believer's confidence in present conflicts.

The Adversary cannot win. His final defeat is not contingent on the outcome of any battle he is currently fighting. His final defeat was set at the cross. It will be visibly enacted at the time God has appointed. Nothing he does now changes that. He may feel the trajectory accelerating. He may strike with the desperation of the doomed. But he cannot escape what is coming. He is a defeated being on his way to a settled end, and every move he makes brings him closer to it.

For the believer, this should be extremely settling. The conflict we face is real, but the outcome is decided. The Adversary cannot win against the One who has already defeated him. He cannot win against the believer who is hidden in the One who has defeated him. The believer's victory is guaranteed by Christ's victory. The two are inseparable. To defeat the believer would require defeating Christ first, and Christ has already settled that question by walking out of the tomb.

How the Cross Answers Each of the Adversary's Roles

Look at how the cross answers each of the names and titles that I introduced in Chapter Three. The portrait of the Adversary in Scripture is built from those titles. The cross addresses every one of them.

The Adversary, the one who opposes, was opposed at the cross. He brought his full force against the Son of God. He used the Roman authorities, the religious leadership, the betrayal of one his disciples, the denial of another, the desertion of the rest, the mockery of the crowds. He pressed every advantage. He was defeated. The Adversary's opposition reached its climax at the cross and was answered there definitively. Every subsequent opposition is the work of an opponent who has already lost his decisive battle.

The Accuser, the one who brings charges against the brethren, has had his case dismantled. The charges he brings against believers are real charges. The believers have fallen short and continue to do so. They have done what he says they have done. But the cross has paid the price for those sins. The accusations now fall in a court that has already issued the verdict. He still throws the charges. They no longer land where they used to land. Romans 8:33 names this directly: *"Who shall lay any thing to the charge of God's elect? It is God that justifieth."*

The Devil, the slanderer, the speaker of lies about God's character, has been answered by the cross's display of God's character. The Adversary said God was withholding good from humanity. The cross showed God giving the highest good He could give: His own Son. The Adversary said God's commands were oppressive. The cross showed God paying the cost of His own commands so that those who broke them could be restored. Every slander the Adversary has ever spoken about God's character has been refuted by what God did at Calvary. The believer who has the cross in view cannot be moved by accusations against God's character.

The Father of Lies has been answered by the truth. Jesus said in John 14:6, *"I am the way, the truth, and the life."* The truth incarnate (in the flesh) stood against the lie at the cross and triumphed. Every lie the Adversary tells now exists in a world where the Truth has spoken and risen. The lies still get told. They no longer have the field to themselves.

The Murderer, the one who brought death into the world through the lie in Eden, has been answered by the resurrection. The murderer's primary work is undone whenever a person passes from death to life through Christ. Every conversion is a resurrection in miniature. Every believer who walks in newness of life is a living refutation of the murderer's claim that his work is final.

The Roaring Lion, the open attacker who tries to devour believers, has been answered by the Lion of the tribe of Judah, who has prevailed (Revelation 5:5). There is a Lion who outranks the lion who roars. The believer who has fled to the Lion of Judah cannot be devoured by the lion of the Adversary's account.

The Ancient Serpent, the subtle deceiver, has had his head crushed at the cross, exactly as Genesis 3:15 promised. He still slithers. He no longer rules.

Every name of the Adversary has has been answered. The believer who walks in view of the cross has the answer to each one already in their hands.

The Believer's Outcome

The practical effect of all of this should now be clear. The believer who has internalized the already-defeated truth lives in a different way than the believer who has not.

We pray **with confidence**, because we are praying to the Father of the Risen Son who has already defeated the enemy.

We resist temptation **with confidence**, because the One who tempts us is a defeated being whose offers have been exposed as bankrupt.

We share the gospel **with confidence,** because the message we carry is the announcement of a victory that has already been won, not the proposal of a campaign whose outcome is uncertain.

We face persecution **with confidence,** because the worst that opposition can do to us was already done to Christ, and He walked out of it on the third day.

We face death **with confidence**, because the power of death has been broken at the cross, and our death will be a passage into the visible presence of the One who already defeated death on us behalf.

This confidence is not bravado. It is sober trust in what Scripture has actually said about what Christ has actually done. The believer who has caught it walks differently, prays differently, shares the Gospel differently, and dies differently than the believer who has not. The doctrine of the already-defeated Adversary is not a piece of information. It is the foundation of the Christian's influence in the world.

What This Chapter Establishes

One. Genesis 3:15 announces the Adversary's defeat in the same scene as the Fall. The contest's outcome was named before the human race had even been expelled from the garden.

Two. Colossians 2:13-15 describes the cross as a Roman triumphal procession in which the principalities and powers were stripped, paraded, and publicly humiliated.

Three. Hebrews 2:14-15 says Christ destroyed the one who had the power of death by means of His own death, delivering believers from the lifelong fear of death that was the Adversary's leverage over them.

Four. 1 John 3:8 says the Son of God was manifested to destroy the works of the Devil. This destruction is in continuous progress and includes the believer's participation.

Five. The believer lives in the "already and not yet." The decisive victory is won. The full visible manifestation is still future. We stand in occupied territory whose liberation is settled.

Six. Romans 8:37 says believers are *"more than conquerors"* (*hupernikao*). The exaggerated language captures the asymmetry of a contest whose outcome is no longer in doubt.

Seven. Revelation 20:10 describes the Adversary's final destination in the lake of fire. The trajectory is fixed. The end is certain.

Review Questions

1. Genesis 3:15 is sometimes called the *protoevangelium*, the first gospel. What does this passage announce, and why does it matter that the announcement was made in the same scene as the Fall?

2. The chapter describes the asymmetry in Genesis 3:15 between the Serpent's bruising of the Seed's heel and the Seed's bruising of the Serpent's head. How does this asymmetry play out at the cross?

3. Galatians 3:16 confirms that the Seed of the woman is singular, identifying it as Christ. How does this single-Seed reading shape the way we should read the rest of Scripture?

4. Colossians 2:13-15 describes the cross as a Roman triumphal procession. What was a Roman triumph, and how does Paul apply the image to what Christ accomplished?

5. The chapter argues that the cross looks like the Adversary's victory but is actually his public humiliation. How does this reframe what was happening at Calvary?

6. Hebrews 2:14-15 says Christ destroyed the one with the power of death *"through death."* What is strategically significant about Christ defeating the Adversary by dying?

7. The chapter says fear of death runs underneath many of the Adversary's manipulations of believers. How does the cross's answer to death reduce his leverage on the believer's daily decisions?

8. 1 John 3:8 says the Son of God was manifested *"to destroy the works of the devil."* How is this destruction in continuous progress, and how does the believer participate in it?

9. The chapter introduces the "already and not yet" pattern. What is the difference between the decisive victory already accomplished and the full visible manifestation still to come?

10. Ephesians 6:11-13 commands believers to *"stand"* rather than to advance. What does the language of standing assume about the territory the believer occupies?

11. Romans 8:37 uses the Greek *hupernikao*, *"more than conquerors."* Why does the chapter call this *"exaggerated language"* and what does it reveal about the asymmetry of the conflict?

12. Revelation 20:10 fixes the Adversary's final destination as the lake of fire. How does knowing the final outcome change a believer's response to present conflicts?

13. The chapter says the believer's victory is inseparable from Christ's victory because we are hidden in Him. What are the practical implications of this for confidence in spiritual conflict?

14. The chapter ends with five descriptions of how the already-defeated truth changes the believer's posture in prayer, temptation, witness, persecution, and death. Walk through each one and explain how the doctrine produces the posture.

REFERENCES

1. On Genesis 3:15 as the *protoevangelium*, see Gordon J. Wenham, Genesis 1-15, Word Biblical Commentary (Waco: Word Books, 1987).

2. On the Roman triumph and its application to Colossians 2:15, see Peter T. O'Brien, The Letter to the Colossians and to Philemon, New International Greek Testament Commentary (Grand Rapids: Eerdmans, 1982).

3. On Hebrews 2:14-15 and the destruction of the Adversary's power through Christ's death, see Philip Edgcumbe Hughes, A Commentary on the Epistle to the Hebrews (Grand Rapids: Eerdmans, 1977).

4. On 1 John 3:8 and the destruction of the works of the Devil, see I. Howard Marshall, The Epistles of John, New International Commentary on the New Testament (Grand Rapids: Eerdmans, 1978).

5. On the "already and not yet" structure of New Testament eschatology, see George Eldon Ladd, A Theology of the New Testament (Grand Rapids: Eerdmans, 1974).

6. On Revelation 20 and the final defeat of Satan, see G. K. Beale, The Book of Revelation, New International Greek Testament Commentary (Grand Rapids: Eerdmans, 1999).

7. On Romans 8:37 and the meaning of *hupernikao*, see Douglas J. Moo, The Epistle to the Romans, New International Commentary on the New Testament (Grand Rapids: Eerdmans, 1996).

CHAPTER TWELVE

The Armor of God

"Finally, my brethren, be strong in the Lord, and in the power of his might. Put on the whole armour of God, that ye may be able to stand against the wiles of the devil. For we wrestle not against flesh and blood, but against principalities, against powers, against the rulers of the darkness of this world, against spiritual wickedness in high places. Wherefore take unto you the whole armour of God, that ye may be able to withstand in the evil day, and having done all, to stand. Stand therefore, having your loins girt about with truth, and having on the breastplate of righteousness; And your feet shod with the preparation of the gospel of peace; Above all, taking the shield of faith, wherewith ye shall be able to quench all the fiery darts of the wicked. And take the helmet of salvation, and the sword of the Spirit, which is the word of God: Praying always with all prayer and supplication in the Spirit, and watching thereunto with all perseverance and supplication for all saints." (Ephesians 6:10-18)

Paul is closing his letter to the Ephesians. He has spent five and a half chapters establishing the believer's position in Christ. Now he turns to the conflict that believer is in, and he gives us the equipment for standing up in it and through it. The armor of God is not a metaphor for self-improvement. It is the actual provision Christ has made for a real war against a very real enemy. Each piece of this armor has a specific function. Each piece answers a specific attack. Together they form a complete covering for the believer who takes the battle seriously.

The previous chapter established that the Adversary has already been defeated at the cross. This chapter takes up the question of how the believer stands in that already-won victory through the specific equipment the Lord has provided. The ground has been taken. The believer's job is to hold it. We hold it by putting on what Paul tells us to put on, and by doing so with the seriousness the equipment deserves.

A young believer should read this chapter as a practical how-to style manual. The armor is not decorative. It is not poetic. It is the kit that lets us stand against the attacks the previous chapters have described. Temptation, accusation, deception, and the organized work of the devil. Each attack has a countermeasure in this armor. The believer who knows the kit, and uses it, is not the easy target the Adversary is looking for.

The Command to Put It On

Paul's language in Ephesians 6 is not suggestive. Instead it is imperative. *"Put on the whole armour of God." "Take unto you the whole armour of God." "Stand therefore."* The verbs used here are commands. The armor does not put itself on. The believer has to do something. The armor is provided, but the putting on is our active work.

This is important to take note of. A lot of Christian teaching treats spiritual armor as something that is automatically operational in the believer's life as long as we are a Christian. Paul does not describe it that way. He commands specific action. The believer has to choose, repeatedly, daily, to put on each piece. The believer who has not done this is not protected by the armor, even though we have access to it.

The Greek word translated "*whole armour*" is *panoplia*. It refers to the complete set of equipment a Roman soldier wore into battle. The word became the root of the English word *panoply*. Paul is specifying that the armor is a complete set.

Partial armor is not sufficient for the war that the Christian is in. A soldier with a breastplate but no helmet is vulnerable at the head. A soldier with a shield but no sword can defend but not press the fight. The believer needs the whole set. Paul does not give us the option to pick and choose what we want or what we feel like.

The Greek word translated "*stand*" appears four times in this short passage. The command is to stand, then to withstand, then to stand, then to stand. Paul is hammering the verb. He is not telling the believer to charge. He is not telling us to advance. He is telling us to stand. The ground has already been taken by Christ. The believer's job is to refuse to give it up. That is the whole point of this spiritual armor passage. Hold the position Christ has placed you in. Do not retreat. Do not concede. Stand.

The Belt of Truth

> "*Having your loins girt about with truth.*" (Ephesians 6:14)

The Roman soldier's belt was not a fashion item. It was the foundational piece of the kit. The belt held the tunic in place for free movement. It held the scabbard for the sword. It held everything else together. A soldier without a belt was a soldier whose other equipment would fall out of place in the heat of battle.

Paul identifies the belt with truth. This is the believer's integrity that is based 100% on the teachings of truth – scripture (John 17:17). Our inner alignment with what is real. It is our refusal to live a double life or to hide things that ought to be exposed. Truth, in Paul's usage, is not primarily propositional (though it includes the propositions of Scripture). It also is the believer's own honesty before God and before ourselves.

Why is truth the first piece? Because the Adversary's primary weapon is deception, and deception works through what is hidden. The believer who is living with hidden sins, hidden compromises, hidden deceptions about our own situation, has taken off the belt. The rest of the armor cannot be held in place without it. The other pieces depend on the first.

A young believer should take this seriously. Put on the belt by getting honest. Get honest with God first. Tell Him what you are actually doing, actually feeling, actually tempted by. Get honest with a trusted mature believer second. The sin that has been named out loud in the presence of another believer has lost most of its power. It cannot hide anymore. The belt has been put on. Everything else becomes easier.

1 John 1:7-9 gives the practice:

> *"If we walk in the light, as he is in the light, we have fellowship one with another, and the blood of Jesus Christ his Son cleanseth us from all sin...If we confess our sins, he is faithful and just to forgive us our sins, and to cleanse us from all unrighteousness."*

Walking in the light is the practice of the belt. It is the believer keeping short accounts with God and refusing to let anything hide.

The Breastplate of Righteousness

> *"And having on the breastplate of righteousness."* (Ephesians 6:14)

The Roman breastplate protected the vital organs. The heart and the lungs. The parts of the body where a wound was fatal. Paul identifies this protection with righteousness.

This is the believer's actual daily obedience. Our living in line with what God has commanded. This practical righteousness does not earn our standing with God (that is settled by the death of Jesus), but it protects us from the vulnerabilities that compromise creates. The believer who has been walking in known, unconfessed sin has gaps in our breastplate. Those gaps are exactly where the Adversary's arrows will land.

This practical righteousness is the keeping of the breastplate in good repair. The obedience to God and His Word is the maintenance of this armor.

The Shoes of the Gospel of Peace

> *"And your feet shod with the preparation of the gospel of peace."* (Ephesians 6:15)

The Roman soldier's footwear was specially designed for stability in battle. The sole often had nails driven through it to grip the ground. A soldier could plant his feet and not be pushed back. The word translated *"preparation"* suggests a readiness. Paul identifies the shoes with the gospel of peace, in a position of readiness.

Two dimensions of this piece matter. The first is stability. The believer who is grounded in the gospel has a place to stand. The peace with God that the gospel provides (Romans 5:1) is the ground under our feet. We are not slipping. We are not being pushed back. The gospel holds us in place.

The second is readiness to carry the gospel to others. The shoes prepare us to move. Isaiah 52:7 says, *"How beautiful upon the mountains are the feet of him that bringeth good tidings, that publisheth peace."* The believer is not just standing. We are ready to move toward the unbeliever with the message of reconciliation. The posture is defensive in one sense and offensive in another. We hold our ground. We also carry the gospel to those who are still in the Adversary's territory.

Every Christian should think about what the gospel shoes look like in our lives. Are we grounded? Do we know where we stand with God? Can we articulate the gospel to someone who has never heard it? If we cannot, the shoes are not fully on. The remedy is to rehearse the gospel until we can speak it clearly and confidently.

1 Peter 3:15 says to "*be ready always to give an answer to every man that asketh you a reason of the hope that is in you.*" Ready. The readiness is the shoes.

The Shield of Faith

> "*Above all, taking the shield of faith, wherewith ye shall be able to quench all the fiery darts of the wicked.*" (Ephesians 6:16)

The Greek word translated "*shield*" here is *thureos*. This was not the small round shield some Roman soldiers carried. It was the large rectangular shield, about four feet tall and two and a half feet wide, that a soldier could hide behind almost entirely. The *thureos* was covered in leather that could be soaked in water before battle. When flaming arrows were shot at the shield, the water-soaked leather extinguished them on contact.

Paul identifies this piece with faith. He specifies the attacks it answers: the fiery darts of the wicked. These are the thoughts, accusations, doubts, and temptations that the Adversary shoots into the believer's mind. Sudden intrusive thoughts. Unexplained surges of fear, lust, or anger. Persistent accusations that do not match our actual situation. These are fiery darts, and they are real.

Faith is the shield. Not faith in the abstract. Not just "believing really hard." Faith in the specific truths God has revealed about Himself, about the believer's standing in Christ, about the Adversary's defeat, about the final outcome of the contest. The believer who is facing a fiery dart answers it with the truth we have been taught. The dart meets the shield. The water-soaked leather of faith extinguishes it.

The phrase "above all" in Paul's list is noteworthy. He does not mean the shield is more important than the other pieces. He means the shield is carried in addition to them, and it covers the areas the other pieces do not reach. The belt, breastplate, and shoes cover the torso and feet. The helmet covers the head. The shield covers everything else, by being movable. Wherever the attack is coming from, the shield can be positioned to answer it. Faith, in the same way, is not attached to one area of the believer's life. It moves. It covers whatever is being attacked at the moment.

The Helmet of Salvation

> *"And take the helmet of salvation."* (Ephesians 6:17)

The helmet protects the head. The mind. The area where the Adversary does most of his work in every believer's life. Thoughts of doubt. Thoughts of despair. Thoughts of worthlessness. Thoughts that contradict what Scripture has said is true. All of these are attacks on the head. The helmet answers and protects them.

Paul identifies the helmet with salvation. Salvation is not just the past event of the believer's conversion. It is the comprehensive work of God that includes the believer's past (justification), our present (sanctification), and our future (glorification). All three are packed into the word. The helmet is the believer's grip on this comprehensive salvation.

When the Adversary attacks the mind with the thought "you are not saved, you have lost your salvation, you were never really saved in the first place," the helmet is the answer. The believer's salvation does not depend on us current feelings. It does not depend on us perfect performance. It depends on what God has done, is doing, and will do. That is a triple foundation. It cannot be moved by the feelings of any given day.

1 Thessalonians 5:8 adds a nuance to the helmet. Paul calls it *"for an helmet, the hope of salvation."* The helmet is not just the fact of salvation but the hope of it. The forward-looking expectation. The believer who has our eyes fixed on the completion of what God has begun is wearing the helmet. We are not moved by present circumstances, because we know where we are going. The hope is protective. It keeps the mind steady.

The Sword of the Spirit

> *"And the sword of the Spirit, which is the word of God."* (Ephesians 6:17)

The sword is the only offensive piece in the list. Paul identifies it as the word of God. The Greek word translated "word" here is *rhema*, meaning the specific spoken word, the particular Scripture applied to the particular situation. This is not just the Bible in general. It is the specific verse, the specific truth, spoken in the moment it is needed.

Jesus modeled this in His wilderness temptation. When the Adversary tempted Him, Jesus answered each temptation with a specific Scripture. Not a general principle. Not a pious thought. A specific verse, spoken into the specific attack. "It is written...It is written...It is written." Three times. Three swords.

This is why memorization of Scripture is not optional for the believer who intends to stand. The verses we know by heart are the ones available to us in the moment of attack. The verses we have only heard about are not. When the fiery dart of temptation comes at two in the morning, the believer does not have time to look up the answer. The answer has to already be in us.

A young believer should take this very practically. Memorize verses. Not just verses that comfort us. Verses that answer specific attacks. Verses that answer accusation (Romans 8:33-34). Verses that answer temptation (1 Corinthians 10:13). Verses that answer doubt (2 Timothy 1:12). Verses that answer fear (2 Timothy 1:7). Verses that answer despair (Romans 8:28). Each one is a sword stroke. Each one is the *rhema* of God, applied to the specific situation.

The Hebrews 4:12 description of the sword is direct:

> "For the word of God is quick, and powerful, and sharper than any twoedged sword, piercing even to the dividing asunder of soul and spirit, and of the joints and marrow, and is a discerner of the thoughts and intents of the heart."

The word cuts. It goes deep. It discerns. It exposes. This is the offensive equipment the believer has been given. Nothing else in our spiritual kit does what the sword does.

Prayer as the Atmosphere

> *"Praying always with all prayer and supplication in the Spirit, and watching thereunto with all perseverance and supplication for all saints."* (Ephesians 6:18)

Paul does not list prayer as a seventh piece of armor. He lists it as something different. The armor is worn. The prayer is the atmosphere in which the armor is worn. Each piece of the armor is put on in the context of continuous communion with God through prayer.

The Greek word for *"perseverance"* is *proskartereo*, meaning to persist, to continue steadfastly, to devote oneself to a thing. The believer is called to pray with this kind of sustained attention. Not prayer as occasional events. Prayer as the continuous background of our lives. The armor is put on in the morning. The prayer continues throughout the day.

Paul specifies what kind of prayer. *"All prayer and supplication in the Spirit."* All kinds of prayer. Worship. Confession. Thanksgiving. Intercession. Request. All of them, continuously, as the breathing of the spiritual life.

He also specifies the object. *"Supplication for all saints."* The believer's prayer is not just for ourselves. It is for the whole body of Christ. The armor is individual. The prayer is corporate. The believer stands in our own armor, but we hold up other believers in prayer as they stand in theirs. No one is standing alone. The whole church is standing together, each in our own place, all covering each other in prayer.

This is the reason the church matters so much in the believer's life. The Adversary works to isolate believers, because an isolated believer is easier prey. The prayer of the saints for each other is one of the main ways the church stays together in the face of this pressure. The believer who has been prayed for by other believers that morning is standing in more than our own armor. We are standing in the collective resistance of the body of Christ.

Putting On the Armor in Practice

How does a young believer actually put on the armor? Here are the practical steps.

First, do it deliberately. Do not assume the armor is on because you are a Christian. Put it on. Morning by morning, if not more often. Name the pieces to yourself. Walk through them.

Belt of truth. Am I living in honesty before God today? Are there any hidden things I need to bring into the light? Confess anything that surfaces. Walk in truth.

Breastplate of righteousness. Am I walking in practical obedience? Where there are gaps, close them. Where there are compromises, repent of them.

Shoes of the gospel of peace. Am I grounded in the gospel? Do I know where I stand with God? Am I ready to share the gospel if the chance comes today? If not, rehearse the basics.

Shield of faith. What am I trusting God for today? What promises of His am I holding on to? Where are the fiery darts likely to come, and what truths will I use to answer them?

Helmet of salvation. Am I grounded in my salvation past, present, and future? Am I remembering the hope set before me? Is my mind being protected from thoughts that contradict what Scripture has established?

Sword of the Spirit. What passages of Scripture do I have available to me today? What specific verses can I use against specific attacks? If the kit is thin, work on filling it.

Prayer. Am I walking in prayer today, or have I started to drift into silence? If silent, start talking again. Prayer for myself. Prayer for others.

This is not a magical ritual. It is a practice. Done every day, it forms habits that make standing in spiritual conflict the default, not the occasional effort. The believer who has been putting on the armor daily for five years is a different believer from the one who has been hoping the armor was somehow on by itself.

The Armor and the Already-Defeated Enemy

One more observation before closing the chapter. Why does the believer need armor at all, if the Adversary has already been defeated?

The answer is that the armor is the equipment for standing in the already-won victory. The Adversary has been defeated, but he has not yet been removed from the field. He still shoots fiery darts. He still probes for weaknesses. He still attempts, even though he cannot finally succeed, to move the believer off the ground Christ has given us. The armor is what keeps us from giving up ground that Christ already paid for.

Think of the armor this way. It is not what wins the war. The war has been won. The armor is what keeps the individual believer from being pushed off our post during the mop-up operations. We are not fighting for victory. We are holding a position in a victory that has already been secured. The armor equips us for that holding work.

This is also why the armor does not fail when it is actually used. It has the full weight of Christ's victory behind it. Each piece is an application, to the believer's specific situation, of what Christ has accomplished. The belt is His truth. The breastplate is pursuing His righteousness. The shoes are His gospel. The shield is the faith He has given. The helmet is His salvation. The sword is His word. The prayer is communion with Him through His Spirit. Every piece is Christ, applied in a specific form to a specific area. The armor works because Christ works.

What This Chapter Establishes

One. Ephesians 6:10-18 commands the believer to put on the whole armor of God (*panoplia*). The armor is a complete set. Partial armor is not sufficient.

Two. The command is active. The armor does not put itself on. The believer has to put it on deliberately.

Three. The posture is standing. The ground has been taken by Christ. The believer's job is to hold it.

Four. The six pieces of armor are truth, righteousness, the gospel of peace, faith, salvation, and the word of God. Each answers a specific line of attack.

Five. The sword (*rhema*) is the only offensive piece. It is the specific Scripture applied to the specific situation. Memorization of Scripture is the practical preparation for wielding it.

Six. Prayer (*proskartereo*) is not a seventh piece. It is the atmosphere in which the armor is worn. Continuous, persistent, for self and for other saints.

Seven. The armor is the equipment for standing in the already-won victory. It works because Christ works.

Review Questions

1. Ephesians 6:10-18 repeatedly commands the believer to *"stand."* "What does this verb tell us about the posture the armor is designed for?

2. Paul uses the Greek word *panoplia* (whole armor). Why does he insist on a complete set rather than allowing the believer to pick and choose?

3. The chapter says the armor is not automatically operational in the believer's life. What does this mean, and what is the believer's active role?

4. The belt of truth is the first piece. Why is inner honesty the foundation that holds the rest of the armor in place?

5. 1 John 1:7-9 describes walking in the light and confessing sins. How does this practice correspond to putting on the belt?

6. The breastplate of righteousness has two dimensions: imputed and practical. How do the two kinds of righteousness work together, and what happens when only one is emphasized?

7. The shoes of the gospel of peace have both a stability dimension and a readiness dimension. What does each one look like in the believer's daily life?

8. The Greek word *thureos* describes the large rectangular Roman shield that could be soaked in water to extinguish flaming arrows. How does this image apply to faith answering the Adversary's fiery darts?

9. What are the "fiery darts of the wicked" in the believer's actual experience, and what does it look like to answer them with specific truths from Scripture?

10. The helmet of salvation protects the mind. 1 Thessalonians 5:8 adds that it is *"the hope of salvation."* How do past, present, and future dimensions of salvation work together to guard the believer's thoughts?

11. The sword of the Spirit is identified as the word of God. The Greek word *rhema* means the specific spoken word. Why does this specificity require the

believer to memorize particular passages rather than just have general familiarity with the Bible?

12. Jesus answered each of His three wilderness temptations with a specific Scripture. How does His example model the use of the sword?

13. Prayer is not listed as a seventh piece of armor. The chapter calls it "the atmosphere in which the armor is worn." What does this mean, and how does *proskartereo* (persistent continuance) apply?

14. Paul says the prayer is not only for the self but "for all saints." How does corporate prayer keep the church standing together against the Adversary's effort to isolate believers?

15. The chapter walks through seven practical steps for putting on the armor each morning. Walk through each step and explain how it applies to your own daily life.

REFERENCES

1. On the Ephesians 6 armor passage and its Old Testament background, see Andrew T. Lincoln, Ephesians, Word Biblical Commentary (Dallas: Word Books, 1990).

2. On *panoplia* and the description of Roman military equipment, see Clinton E. Arnold, Ephesians: Power and Magic, Society for New Testament Studies Monograph Series 63 (Cambridge: Cambridge University Press, 1989).

3. On the imputed and practical dimensions of righteousness, see John Murray, Redemption Accomplished and Applied (Grand Rapids: Eerdmans, 1955).

4. On *thureos* and the Roman shield, see Peter T. O'Brien, The Letter to the Ephesians, Pillar New Testament Commentary (Grand Rapids: Eerdmans, 1999).

5. On *rhema* versus logos in Paul's usage, see Gerhard Kittel and Gerhard Friedrich, eds., Theological Dictionary of the New Testament (Grand Rapids: Eerdmans, 1964-1976).

6. On Jesus's use of Scripture in the wilderness temptation, see D. A. Carson, Matthew, Expositor's Bible Commentary (Grand Rapids: Zondervan, 1984).

7. On prayer as *proskartereo* in the Christian life, see D. A. Carson, A Call to Spiritual Reformation: Priorities from Paul and His Prayers (Grand Rapids: Baker, 1992).

CHAPTER THIRTEEN

Victory in Jesus

"But Daniel purposed in his heart that he would not defile himself with the portion of the king's meat, nor with the wine which he drank: therefore he requested of the prince of the eunuchs that he might not defile himself." (Daniel 1:8)

Daniel was a teenager, taken captive to Babylon with the other young noblemen of Judah. He is placed in the royal training program. He is given a new name designed to honor a pagan god. He is placed in a cultural environment designed to absorb him into the service of a foreign empire. At the first moment of compromise, the food from the king's table, he draws the line. Not with drama. Not with public protest. He purposes in his heart. He then makes a quiet, respectful request. The stand is made before the request is ever spoken out loud. The decision is already settled inside him. Everything after is just the working out of what has already been decided.

The previous chapter took up the armor of God as the practical equipment for standing in spiritual conflict. This chapter is the synthesis. It gathers everything this book has taught and looks at what walking in victory actually looks like in the life of a faithful child of God. The book has been building toward this.

Daniel is the anchor because Daniel was young, faithful, and in hostile territory. He is the model for any believer, especially our young Christians, who have to live by faith in an environment that does not share it. Which is to say, every believer reading this chapter. The principles that carried Daniel through Babylon will carry us through whatever setting we find ourselves in. The Adversary's strategies have not changed. Neither has the Lord's provision for those who purpose in their hearts to stand.

Purposing in the Heart

Daniel's stand began with an inside decision. "*Daniel purposed in his heart.*" The Hebrew verb for "purposed" suggests setting something firmly in place. Daniel did not wait until the moment of pressure to decide what he would do. He decided in advance. When the pressure came, he was not surprised by it, and he was not making up his response on the spot.

This is the first principle of walking in victory. The decisions about how you will respond to the Adversary's attacks have to be made before the attacks arrive. The person who waits until the moment of temptation to decide whether they will resist has already lost most of the battle. The emotional pull of the moment, the social pressure, the sudden availability of the forbidden thing, the clever argument that sounds reasonable, all of these are designed to overwhelm a person who is making their decision in real time. The person who has already decided, in advance, is not making a decision in the moment. They are executing a decision that they already made.

We can purpose in our hearts about many things. We can purpose that we will not compromise on sexual purity, regardless of what culture says or what our peers are doing. We can purpose that we will not dishonor our parents in the way our friends do. We can purpose that we will not participate in the entertainment that contradicts what God has said. We can purpose that we will keep our word even when keeping it costs us. We can purpose that we will speak up for Christ when we could have stayed silent. Each of these is a pre-decision. Each of these is a settled position before the pressure ever comes.

The practical effect is real. The believer who has purposed in advance answers pressure with steady resistance rather than internal struggle. Our "no" is calm, not panicked. Our boundaries are clear, not confused. We are harder to move because the decision has already been made. The Adversary's best strategies assume an undecided believer. The believer who has decided is an unusually difficult target.

Submitting and Resisting

James 4:7 gives the two-move answer to the Adversary: *"Submit yourselves therefore to God. Resist the devil, and he will flee from you."*

The order matters. Submission comes first. Resistance comes second. The person who tries to resist the Adversary without submitting to God first is trying to fight a war without authorization from the commanding officer. We have no ground to stand on, because our position has not been surrendered to the One who can hold it.

The Greek word for "*submit*" is *hupotasso*, meaning to arrange under, to place in subjection. It is a military word, describing the arrangement of soldiers under a commander's authority. The believer submits to God by placing ourselves under His authority, His word, His purposes, His timing. This is not a dramatic act. It is the steady daily practice of the Christian life.

The Greek word for "*resist*" is *anthistemi*, meaning to stand against, to set oneself firmly opposed to. It is also a military word. The believer resists the Adversary by refusing to move when he attacks. We do not argue. We do not negotiate. We stand against him.

The promise attached to the resistance is notable. "*He will flee from you.*" The Adversary does not match the believer's resistance with a stronger pressure. He withdraws. This is the inverse of what a young believer might expect. We imagine that resisting would make the attack worse. Scripture says it makes the attack end. The Adversary is not interested in prolonged contests with believers who are not going to yield. He is looking for easier targets. When he finds a believer who has purposed in our hearts and is submitting to God and resisting him, he moves on.

This has been the universal experience of faithful believers across centuries. The attack that seems overwhelming when it first arrives diminishes when it is met with steady resistance. It does not always disappear immediately. Sometimes it goes on for a while. But it diminishes. The believer who holds our ground finds that the pressure we feared would crush us actually recedes, and we are left standing.

Not Ignorant of His Devices

2 Corinthians 2:11 names a quiet principle that has run through this whole book:

> *"Lest Satan should get an advantage of us: for we are not ignorant of his devices."*

The Greek word translated *"devices"* is *noema*, meaning thoughts, designs, schemes, or purposes. Paul assumes believers know what the Adversary's schemes are. He also warns that ignorance of them would give the Adversary an advantage. Being informed is protection. Being uninformed is vulnerability.

This book is an attempt at a response to that principle. Every chapter has been an effort to name what the Adversary actually does and how the believer can recognize it. The biblical picture of the throne and the heavenly order. The fall of Satan and its details. The names and titles that describe his activity. The cultural distortions that have replaced the biblical picture. The disguise as an angel of light. The three-move sequence of temptation. The operation of accusation. The hierarchy of the fallen realm. The limits on what he can do. The cessation of the miraculous period's form of demonic activity. The already-won victory at the cross. The armor for standing in that victory. Each chapter has added another device to the list, and named the biblical response.

Every person who has worked through this material is no longer ignorant. The Adversary has lost one of his major advantages over us. He cannot operate in the shadows because we know to look for him. He cannot use the cultural caricatures because we know what the biblical picture actually is. He cannot use the subtle substitutes because we can tell the difference between the true and the counterfeit. The game board has changed. We are not a naive target anymore.

Nine Situations and the Biblical Response

Look at nine specific situations a Christian can and most likely will face, and the biblical response to each, drawing on what this book has taught.

When we face a question designed to loosen our grip on what Scripture says, we remember the Serpent's first move from Chapter Six and answers with what is written. "Yes, God did say. Here is the verse. I believe what it says."

When we face an internal voice that tells us the consequences God named will not follow, we remember the Adversary's signature use of narrow technicalities and stands on the straightforward reading of Scripture. Proverbs 14:12 applies here. The way that seems right may end in death. We trust God's word over the voice that flatters us.

When we face an offer of something genuinely good through a forbidden route, we remember James 1:17 and refuses. The Father of lights does not withhold good from His children. The distorted offer is always a lie about God's character. The right path to the good thing is obedience, not rebellion.

When we face accusation in the quiet hours of the night, we remember Zechariah 3 and Romans 8:33-34. The filthy garments are real. The blood of Christ has covered them. We are clothed in righteousness through the blood of the Lamb. The court has issued its verdict. The Accuser is throwing paper that nobody is reading.

When we face an attractive teacher, preacher, friend, or even a family members, whose message is almost Christian but off in subtle ways, we remember 2 Corinthians 11:14. The angel-of-light disguise is the Adversary's primary mode. We compare what the teacher says to Scripture. Where they conflict, Scripture wins. We refuse to be swept along by personality.

When we face cultural pressure to adopt the surrounding age's version of what is good, true, or acceptable, we remember Romans 12:2. Do not be conformed. Be transformed by the renewing of the mind. We keep saturating ourselves in the actual Word so that the cultural picture cannot displace what Scripture has established.

When we face fear of what we might lose by standing with Christ, we remember Hebrews 2:14-15. The power of death has been broken. Christ has freed us from the fear that was the Adversary's leverage over our whole life. The losses we are being threatened with are survivable. The One who died for us is for us.

When we face discouragement because the fight seems endless and our progress seems small, we remember Ephesians 6:13. "Having done all, to stand." We are not called to advance. We are called to stand. The victory has already been won. Our faithfulness in holding our position is the fullness of what the Lord has asked of us.

When we face the suggestion that our individual obedience does not matter because we are just one person in a large world, we remember that Daniel was just one person in a large empire, and that the Lord used his quiet faithfulness to preserve His people and prepare the way for the Messiah. Our obedience is not small. The scale of what the Lord will do through a faithful believer is not measurable by our own perception in the moment.

Nine situations. Nine responses. All of them drawn from what this book has taught. All of them doable by every believer who has purposed in their hearts.

The Role of the Church

The armor chapter ended with prayer as the corporate dimension of the believer's equipment. The church is the corporate dimension of the believer's life. No Christian is meant to walk in victory alone.

Hebrews 10:24-25 says:

> *"And let us consider one another to provoke unto love and to good works; Not forsaking the assembling of ourselves together, as the manner of some is; but exhorting one another: and so much the more, as ye see the day approaching."*

The Greek word translated "*provoke*" is *paroxusmos*, meaning a sharp stimulation or stirring. The word is normally used in a negative sense in Greek (it gives us the English paroxysm). The author of Hebrews uses it in a positive sense. Believers should stir each other up sharply, actively, toward love and good works. This is what the church is for. Not a social club. Not some moral improvement society. A community of believers whose mutual sharpening and stirring keeps each of them walking in what would be impossible alone.

The Adversary works against this. He works to isolate believers, to divide churches, to make gathering difficult, to make other believers seem unnecessary or annoying or wrong. Every one of these pressures is part of his strategy. The believer who has been pulled away from the church has been pulled into exactly the vulnerability he wants us in. The corrective is simple to name and hard to live. Gather. Keep gathering. Gather even when you do not feel like it. Gather with the specific intent of stirring others up toward Christ and being stirred up by them.

A Christian who has built their life around faithful gathering with a biblical local church of Christ has resources the isolated believer does not have. Accountability. Instruction. Prayer. Encouragement. Correction when we are drifting. Mutual stirring toward love and good works. Shepherding from faithful elders. Preaching from sound preachers. These are not nice extras. They are part of the provision the Lord has made for the Christian life. The armor is individual. The prayer surrounding it is corporate. The gathering that contains the prayer is the church. The whole system works together, and taking any part out weakens the rest.

More Than Conquerors

Romans 8:37-39 is one of what I often refer to as the summit passages of the New Testament:

> *"Nay, in all these things we are more than conquerors through him that loved us. For I am persuaded, that neither death, nor life, nor angels, nor principalities, nor powers, nor things present, nor things to come, nor height, nor depth, nor any other creature, shall be able to separate us from the love of God, which is in Christ Jesus our Lord."*

Paul is not writing from a place of theoretical comfort. He wrote this passage while under Roman persecution, facing prison and eventual execution. The believers he was writing to were being dragged out of their homes, thrown into arenas, executed for entertainment. The conditions were as hostile as anything a young Christian today is likely to face. And into those conditions Paul writes this.

"*More than conquerors.*" The Greek word is *hupernikao*, meaning to over-conquer, to win beyond winning. The prefix *huper* means above or beyond. The root word *nikao* means to conquer or overcome. The believer is not just a conqueror. We are beyond a conqueror. The exaggerated language is intentional. It captures the asymmetry of the situation. The believer is on the side that has already won the decisive battle. What happens to us now, however painful, is happening in a contest whose outcome is settled. We cannot lose. Every attack against us is an attack on a member of an army that has already secured its victory.

The list of things that cannot separate us from God's love is sweeping. Death. Life. Angels. Principalities. Powers. Present. Future. Height. Depth. Any creature. Paul is covering every possible category. The heavenly realm. The earthly realm. The forces of the fallen hierarchy. The full sweep of time. The full sweep of space. None of it. Nothing can separate us from the love of God.

Read that through the lens of this book. The same principalities and powers named in Ephesians 6:12 are named here as unable to separate the believer from God's love. The same death the Adversary used as leverage in Hebrews 2:14-15 is named here as powerless to break the connection. The same "*any other creature*" covers the Adversary himself, who is in the end just a created creature. None of them can touch the core fact of the Christian's life. We are loved by God in Christ. No being, no event, no force in the universe can break that connection.

A believer who has truly learned this, believed this, and internalized this, walks differently than a believer who has not. We are not afraid of what might happen. We have already assessed the worst-case scenarios and concluded that they cannot separate us from the love of God. The Adversary's leverage has been removed. We are, in Paul's language, more than a conquerors!.

The Long View

Someone reading this book may feel the weight of the conflict described and wonder if we can stand in it over the long decades of life. The honest answer is yes, but not by our own strength.

The believers who have walked faithfully for fifty or sixty or even one-hundred years did not do it by superhuman willpower. They did it by putting on the armor every day. By gathering with the church every week. By keeping short accounts with God. By memorizing Scripture. By purposing in their hearts. By trusting the One who had purposed in His heart before the foundation of the world to save them.

The walk is long in our minds on this side of time. The enemy is persistent. But the Lord is more persistent. He does not get tired of holding up the believer who is looking to Him. He does not lose interest. He does not misplace us. He carries us through every season we will face, and He brings us to the end.

Philippians 1:6 is the promise:

> *"Being confident of this very thing, that he which hath begun a good work in you will perform it until the day of Jesus Christ."*

The work the Lord began in the believer will be completed. Not by us. By Him. Our job is to keep walking. His job is to keep carrying.

For the young believer reading this chapter, the horizon is long. We are being prepared for decades of standing. The preparation is what this book has been. The standing is what the rest of our lives will be. We do not have to do it perfectly. We have to keep doing it. The Lord will handle the completion.

Fight From Victory, Not ~~for~~ Victory

One of the most important paradigm shifts a young believer needs to make happens in how they think about the nature of the fight itself. The ordinary religious imagination assumes the contest between us and the Adversary is undecided, and that the believer is fighting to win. Scripture says something different. The fight has already been won. The believer is fighting from that victory, not toward it.

This shift changes the emotional tone of the whole Christian life. A soldier fighting in a war whose outcome is uncertain fights with a desperate, anxious edge. Every setback threatens final defeat. Every small loss feels like the whole thing might be unraveling. The stakes of every individual moment feel enormous, because the whole contest might turn on any given encounter.

A soldier fighting in the mop-up operations of a war that has already been won fights with a different disposition. The setbacks are real, but they are not final. The small losses hurt, but they do not threaten the outcome. The stakes of individual moments are real but bounded. The commanding officer is not going to let the final defeat happen, because the final defeat has already been ruled out.

This is the posture Paul describes. The believer is standing in an already-secured victory. Our resistance to the Adversary's attacks is the holding of ground that Christ has already taken. We are not fighting to save ourselves. Christ has saved us. We are not fighting to prove ourselves. Christ has covered us. We are not fighting to earn anything. Christ has earned everything for us. The fight is not for those things. The fight is to keep standing in what we already have.

A young believer who has caught this shift walks through hard days differently than we walked through them before. The hard day is no longer a day when we might lose our salvation, might prove we are not really a Christian, might give up the ground we have been trying to take. The hard day is a day when the Adversary is trying to push us off a position Christ has already given us, and we are holding that position by the grace He has supplied. When the hard day ends, we are still standing where Christ put us, even if we feel battered. The position has not been lost because it was never ours to lose in the first place. It was Christ's, given to us, held by His grace and His love. The Adversary can bruise the heel. He cannot take the head.

The Quiet Work

Much of what this book has described will never be visible to anyone but us. Our purposing in our hearts will not announce itself. Our putting on of the armor will happen in our bedroom before we leave in the morning. Our resistance to the Adversary's attacks will happen inside our thoughts, in moments no one else witnesses. Our memorization of Scripture will happen in quiet minutes scattered throughout our week. Our prayer for other believers will happen when we are alone.

This quiet work is the bulk of the Christian life. The dramatic moments, when they come, are brief. The quiet, faithful, hidden work of ordinary obedience fills the years between them. The believer who has built our lives around this quiet work is prepared for whatever dramatic moments the Lord brings, because the preparation has been happening all along.

The Adversary knows this. He works hardest at the quiet places, because he knows that the dramatic moments are won or lost in the years that preceded them. The believer who has been sloppy in their private devotional life will be sloppy in their public stand. The believer who has been rigorous in the quiet will be rigorous in the crisis. The Adversary tries to discourage the quiet work precisely because it is where the war is being won, long before anyone sees the visible victories.

Every young Christian should take encouragement from this. The work we are doing that no one sees is the most important work we are doing. The morning prayer no one knows about. The verse we whisper to ourselves while walking between classes. The decision to not look at the thing we are tempted to look at. The apology to our sibling that no one outside our house heard. The choice to forgive a friend who does not know we were tempted not to. Every one of these is a hidden victory. Every one of these is a thread in the rope that will hold us when the large test comes.

The Lord sees all of it. Hebrews 6:10 says,

> *"For God is not unrighteous to forget your work and labour of love, which ye have shewed toward his name."*

Nothing done for Christ is forgotten. Nothing is wasted. The small, hidden work of the young believer is seen and remembered and credited. On the day of Christ's return, every quiet act of faithfulness will be brought to light. The believer who has been faithful in what seemed small will find that what seemed small was actually where the most important part of our lives took place.

May God bless each and everyone of us as we strive to resist the Devil.

What This Chapter Establishes

One. Daniel 1:8 shows the foundational principle of walking in victory: purposing in the heart in advance of the pressure. The decision is made before the attack. The response is not improvised.

Two. James 4:7 gives the two-move answer: submit to God, resist the Devil. The order matters. Submission first, resistance second. The promise is that the Devil flees.

Three. 2 Corinthians 2:11 assumes the believer knows the Adversary's devices. This whole book has been the cataloging of those devices and the biblical responses to them.

Four. Nine specific situations a young believer will face each have a biblical response drawn from earlier chapters. The responses are not improvised. They are the application of what Scripture has already established.

Five. Hebrews 10:24-25 commands the corporate practice of gathering for the mutual stirring up of believers toward love and good works. The Adversary works to isolate. The church is the answer to the isolation.

Six. Romans 8:37-39 establishes that no force in the universe can separate the believer from the love of God in Christ. The believer is "more than a conqueror" (hupernikao) through the One who loved us.

Seven. Philippians 1:6 gives the long view. The work the Lord began in the believer will be completed by Him. Our job is to keep walking. The completion is His.

Review Questions

1. Daniel 1:8 says Daniel *"purposed in his heart"* not to defile himself. Why does the chapter identify this as the first principle of walking in victory, and how does pre-deciding affect the believer's response to pressure?

2. The chapter gives examples of things a young believer can purpose in our hearts about in advance. What does purposing in advance actually look like in a young believer's daily life?

3. James 4:7 gives the two-move sequence: submit to God, resist the Devil. Why does the order matter, and what happens when a believer tries to resist without first submitting?

4. The Greek words *hupotasso* (submit) and *anthistemi* (resist) are both military terms. How does the military language shape the way we should understand these commands?

5. James 4:7 promises that the Devil will flee when resisted. What does this teach about the Adversary's interest in prolonged contests with resistant believers?

6. 2 Corinthians 2:11 assumes believers know the Adversary's devices (*noema*). How does knowledge of his schemes function as practical protection, and what has this book been doing to build that knowledge?

7. The chapter walks through nine specific situations a young believer will face and the biblical response to each. Pick three situations and explain how the response draws on earlier chapters of this book.

8. Hebrews 10:24-25 uses the Greek word *paroxusmos* for *"provoke."* What does it mean that believers should stir each other up sharply toward love and good works?

9. Why does the Adversary work to isolate believers, and how does faithful church gathering answer this strategy?

10. Romans 8:37 says believers are *"more than conquerors"* (*hupernikao*) through Christ. How does the exaggerated language capture the asymmetry of the spiritual conflict?

11. Romans 8:38-39 lists the forces that cannot separate the believer from the love of God. Why does Paul's sweeping list connect to the principalities and powers of Ephesians 6:12 and to the power of death in Hebrews 2:14-15?

12. Philippians 1:6 says the Lord will complete the work He began in the believer. How does this verse support the long view of the Christian walk, and how does it distribute the responsibility between the believer and the Lord?

13. The chapter closes the book with seven final points that gather what has been taught throughout. Walk through each one and explain how it applies to your own life.

14. Looking back at all thirteen chapters, what is the single biggest change in how you think about the Devil now compared to how you thought about him when you started reading?

REFERENCES

1. On Daniel 1:8 and the language of purposing in the heart, see Joyce G. Baldwin, Daniel, Tyndale Old Testament Commentaries (Downers Grove: IVP Academic, 1978).

2. On James 4:7 and the two-move sequence of submit and resist, see Peter H. Davids, The Epistle of James, New International Greek Testament Commentary (Grand Rapids: Eerdmans, 1982).

3. On *hupotasso* and *anthistemi* as military vocabulary, see Gerhard Kittel and Gerhard Friedrich, eds., Theological Dictionary of the New Testament (Grand Rapids: Eerdmans, 1964-1976).

4. On 2 Corinthians 2:11 and awareness of the Adversary's schemes, see Philip Edgcumbe Hughes, Paul's Second Epistle to the Corinthians, New International Commentary on the New Testament (Grand Rapids: Eerdmans, 1962).

5. On Hebrews 10:24-25 and *paroxusmos*, see F. F. Bruce, The Epistle to the Hebrews, New International Commentary on the New Testament (Grand Rapids: Eerdmans, 1990).

6. On Romans 8:37-39 and *hupernikao*, see Douglas J. Moo, The Epistle to the Romans, New International Commentary on the New Testament (Grand Rapids: Eerdmans, 1996).

7. On Philippians 1:6 and the promise of completion, see Peter T. O'Brien, The Epistle to the Philippians, New International Greek Testament Commentary (Grand Rapids: Eerdmans, 1991).

8. On the book of Daniel as a model for faithful young believers in a hostile culture, see Tremper Longman III, Daniel, NIV Application Commentary (Grand Rapids: Zondervan, 1999).

Appendix A: Key Scripture Reference Sheet

This reference sheet organizes the primary Scripture passages cited throughout this book by topic. All quotations are from the King James Version.

The Heavenly Order

"Holy, holy, holy, is the LORD of hosts: the whole earth is full of his glory." (Isaiah 6:3)

"For by him were all things created, that are in heaven, and that are in earth, visible and invisible, whether they be thrones, or dominions, or principalities, or powers: all things were created by him, and for him." (Colossians 1:16)

"Are they not all ministering spirits, sent forth to minister for them who shall be heirs of salvation?" (Hebrews 1:14)

Satan's Origin and Fall

"I beheld Satan as lightning fall from heaven." (Luke 10:18)

"Lest being lifted up with pride he fall into the condemnation of the devil." (1 Timothy 3:6)

"And there was war in heaven: Michael and his angels fought against the dragon... And the great dragon was cast out, that old serpent, called the Devil, and Satan, which deceiveth the whole world: he was cast out into the earth, and his angels were cast out with him." (Revelation 12:7, 9)

Satan's Names and Functions

"Your adversary the devil, as a roaring lion, walketh about, seeking whom he may devour." (1 Peter 5:8)

"He was a murderer from the beginning, and abode not in the truth, because there is no truth in him." (John 8:44)

"The accuser of our brethren is cast down, which accused them before our God day and night." (Revelation 12:10)

"Satan himself is transformed into an angel of light." (2 Corinthians 11:14)

His Strategy and His Limits

"Now the serpent was more subtil than any beast of the field which the LORD God had made." (Genesis 3:1)

"Behold, all that he hath is in thy power; only upon himself put not forth thine hand." (Job 1:12)

"Greater is he that is in you, than he that is in the world." (1 John 4:4)

His Defeat

"And I will put enmity between thee and the woman, and between thy seed and her seed; it shall bruise thy head, and thou shalt bruise his heel." (Genesis 3:15)

"Having spoiled principalities and powers, he made a shew of them openly, triumphing over them in it." (Colossians 2:15)

"Through death he might destroy him that had the power of death, that is, the devil." (Hebrews 2:14)

"The devil that deceived them was cast into the lake of fire and brimstone." (Revelation 20:10)

Spiritual Warfare and Resistance

"Put on the whole armour of God, that ye may be able to stand against the wiles of the devil." (Ephesians 6:11)

"Submit yourselves therefore to God. Resist the devil, and he will flee from you." (James 4:7)

"They overcame him by the blood of the Lamb, and by the word of their testimony." (Revelation 12:11)

"Neither death, nor life, nor angels, nor principalities, nor powers... shall be able to separate us from the love of God, which is in Christ Jesus our Lord." (Romans 8:38-39)

Appendix B: Glossary of Key Terms

The following terms appear throughout this book. Where relevant, their Hebrew, Greek, or Latin origins are given.

Anthistemi Greek: to stand against, to set oneself firmly in opposition. Used in James 4:7 and 1 Peter 5:9 for the believer's resistance of the Adversary.

Archai (Principalities) Greek: beginning, first in rank. Used in Ephesians 6:12 and Colossians 2:15 as a category of fallen spiritual beings in the demonic hierarchy.

Arum Hebrew: crafty, shrewd, clever. Used in Genesis 3:1 to describe the Serpent as *"more subtil"* than any other creature. Not inherently negative, but here in service of deception.

Belial Hebrew: worthlessness, one who brings ruin. Used in 2 Corinthians 6:15 as a title for Satan in direct contrast to Christ.

Cherubim Hebrew plural of cherub. The highest order of created angelic beings in the immediate presence of God's glory. Associated with guarding the tree of life (Genesis 3:24) and the divine throne (Ezekiel 1, 10). The anointed covering cherub of Ezekiel 28:14 is the pre-fall description that may apply to Satan.

Daimonizomai Greek: to be demonized, to be under the control of a demon. The actual word used in New Testament accounts of demonic possession, more precise than the English "possession."

Diabolos Greek: slanderer, false Accuser. The primary New Testament title for Satan, from which the English "devil" is derived. Describes his function as one who throws accusations between people and before God.

Ha-Satan Hebrew: the Adversary. Used with the definite article in Job 1-2 as a title describing a function (opposing, accusing) rather than a personal name.

Helel Hebrew: shining one, brilliant one. Appears only once in the Hebrew Old Testament (Isaiah 14:12), rendered Lucifer in the Latin Vulgate and the KJV. Not a personal name for Satan.

Hupernikao Greek: to have an overwhelming victory, to conquer abundantly. Used in Romans 8:37 to describe believers as *"more than conquerors"* through Christ.

Hupotasso Greek: to place oneself under the authority of another. Used in James 4:7 for the submission to God that precedes and enables resistance to the Adversary.

Kosmokratores Greek: rulers of the darkness of this world. Appears only once in the New Testament (Ephesians 6:12). Describes fallen spiritual beings exercising authority over large domains of the fallen world order.

Luo Greek: to loose, to dissolve, to undo. Used in 1 John 3:8 to describe Christ's purpose: to destroy (undo) the works of the Devil.

Malak / Angelos Hebrew (*malak*) and Greek (*angelos*): messenger. The functional term used for angelic beings throughout both testaments, describing their primary role rather than their nature.

Noema Greek: thought, mental scheme. Used in 2 Corinthians 2:11 for the Adversary's *"devices,"* the schemes he has thought through in advance.

Panoplia Greek: full armor, the complete armor set. Used in Ephesians 6:11 and 6:13 for the whole armor of God, not a partial selection.

Protoevangelium Latin: first gospel. The theological term for Genesis 3:15, God's pronouncement to the Serpent that the seed of the woman would bruise his head. The first announcement of Christ's ultimate victory over the Adversary.

Rhema Greek: spoken word, specific word applied to a specific situation. Used in Ephesians 6:17 for the sword of the Spirit, distinguishing the Bible as specifically applied from the Bible in general.

Saraph Hebrew: burning or fiery one. The root of "seraphim," the heavenly beings surrounding the throne of God in Isaiah 6.

Sulagogeo Greek: to carry off as plunder, to take captive. Used in Colossians 2:8 for the capture of a person's mind by ways of thinking not rooted in Christ.

Thureos Greek: the large Roman door-shield, approximately four feet tall and two and a half feet wide, soaked in water to extinguish incendiary arrows. Referenced in Ephesians 6:16 as the shield of faith.

Appendix C: Recommended Reading

The following resources are recommended for further study, organized by category.

On the Biblical Theology of Satan and Spiritual Warfare

Sydney H. T. Page, Powers of Evil: A Biblical Study of Satan and Demons (Baker, 1995). The best single scholarly treatment of the biblical material on Satan and demons. Careful, evangelical, and honest about interpretive difficulties. Start here.

Clinton E. Arnold, Powers of Darkness: Principalities and Powers in Paul's Letters (IVP Academic, 1992). The standard scholarly treatment of Ephesians 6:12 and the Pauline spiritual warfare passages.

Merrill F. Unger, Biblical Demonology (Kregel, 1994). A thorough treatment of demonic activity in Scripture from a conservative evangelical perspective.

On the Cultural and Historical Development of Satan's Image

Jeffrey Burton Russell, four-volume series: The Devil (1977), Satan (1981), Lucifer (1984), Mephistopheles (1986). All published by Cornell University Press. The definitive scholarly history of how the popular image of Satan developed from antiquity through the modern world.

Darren Oldridge, The Devil: A Very Short Introduction (Oxford University Press, 2012). A concise and readable overview.

On Spiritual Warfare and Practical Resistance

C. S. Lewis, The Screwtape Letters (1942). Fiction, but theologically perceptive. Lewis's imagined correspondence between a senior and junior demon remains one of the most practically insightful treatments of how temptation actually works. Worth reading slowly.

On Job and the Heavenly Court

John E. Hartley, The Book of Job, New International Commentary on the Old Testament (Eerdmans, 1988). The standard evangelical commentary on Job. Essential for understanding the Job 1-2 heavenly court scene.

Thank You for Reading

Thank you for reading this book. I am grateful you gave it your time, and I pray it has been of help to you in some way.

I am always glad to hear from my readers. If you have a question, or if something in these pages stirred a thought you want to talk through, please reach out. I want to communicate with the people who read my work, and I will do my best to answer.

If this book helped you, I would ask one favor. Would you leave an honest five-star review on Amazon? It does more than you might think. A good review helps other people find the book, and it helps me keep writing and put solid material into more hands.

I would also invite you to visit my website at www.gagecoldwater.com. There you will find all of my books gathered in one place, along with many other resources. While you are there, you can sign up for my newsletter. That is the best way to know as soon as I release a new book or new content.

Thank you again for reading.

Gage Coldwater

www.ingramcontent.com/pod-product-compliance
Lightning Source LLC
LaVergne TN
LVHW010655110826
845149LV00014B/3094

* 9 7 9 8 9 9 5 3 7 9 2 3 2 *